Knitted Pirates,
Princesses,
Witches, Wizards
& Fairies

Dedicated to Dossie.
This is for you, mum.

Knitted Pirates, Princesses, Witches, Wizards & Fairies

with outfits & accessories

ANNETTE HEFFORD

Search Press

First published in Great Britain 2010

Search Press Limited
Wellwood, North Farm Road,
Tunbridge Wells, Kent TN2 3DR

Text copyright © Annette Hefford 2010

Photographs by Roddy Paine Photographic Studio

Photographs and design copyright © Search Press Ltd. 2010

ISBN: 978-1-84448-424-9

The Publishers and author can accept no responsibility for any
consequences arising from the information, advice or instructions given
in this publication.

Suppliers
If you have difficulty in obtaining any of the materials and equipment
mentioned in this book, then please visit the Search Press website for
details of suppliers: www.searchpress.com

Printed in Malaysia.

Front cover

Main image: Alistair Wizard, see page 70.

Page 1

Samuel Crowe Pirate, see page 56.

Page 2

Alistair Wizard, see page 70.

Page 3

Princess Neridah, see page 86.

Page 5

Elizabeth Witch (shown actual size), see page 22.

Acknowledgements

*When Daisy Livingstone was finished, the first 'wow'
came from my dear friend and neighbour,
Lorraine Muir. Thanks Lorraine, your 'wow' told me
that I was on the right track.*

*I would never have known if my hieroglyphics would
be understood by other knitters without the help of
my sister, Rosemary Kramer, who knitted up Princess
Neridah in her own special colours and trims and who
did this project using the roughest of draft patterns.
Thank you, dear sister. Thank you also to Julia Powell,
my elder sister, who kindly supplied me with English
yarns so that I could test out tensions and patterns.*

*For their support and encouragement over the last few
years, many thanks to Thelma Douglas and Valerie
Hutchings. You confirmed my dream and helped me to
maintain the excitement when the going got tough.*

*A special thank you to young Sam MacFaull who gave
me the insight into the imaginations of boys and their
love of enchanted pirates.*

*Last but never least, many thanks to all friends
and colleagues who constantly checked on the
book's progress and recharged my enthusiasm over
the years.*

Contents

The Dolls

Introduction

Knitting has always been an enjoyable experience for me, but no craft has given me more pleasure or fun-loving challenges than the contents of this book. It is a joy to share these fantasy dolls, each standing 45cm (18in) tall, knowing that creative knitters everywhere will be rewarded as I have with the appreciative exclamations and smiles of recipients of all ages.

The yarns used to knit these magical characters are widely available. The patterns are easy to follow, with clear instructions and photographs. Each of the enchanting dolls are described in their own chapters so as to inspire the imagination of both knitter and child.

I hope that you will enjoy the challenge of detailed work using smaller-sized needles to complete the delightful details, and the fun of adding embellishments and extra sparkle. Simply changing yarn colours can create a completely different doll, which I am sure will encourage you, as it did me, to picture and make a variety of very special and uniquely crafted characters.

The timeless appeal of these loveable figures make them suitable for children and adults alike; boys as well as girls. If treasured and cared for, they can be passed on as gifts to the next generation – an heirloom for future children and grandchildren to enjoy! They will cast a spell on you, and on their lucky recipients, providing many hours of make-believe and creative playtime.

Dressable dolls have always been winners, and all the clothes and accessories featured in the book are interchangeable – I am sure, for example, that Elizabeth Witch would love a pair of sandals like those of Alistair Wizard to wear on hot summer days, or a pretty pair of shoes like Princess Neridah's for those special parties. Indeed, there is no reason why all the clothes could not be adapted to fit a child's favourite doll. Prepare to knit your own magical world – and not a battery in sight!

Equipment & materials

You need very little in the way of equipment to knit the dolls in this book, and most of the items you will probably already have in your workbasket. I have listed everything you need at the start of each project, including the approximate amounts of each colour yarn required, but feel free to alter these to use up oddments you may have stored away at home, and to stamp your own character on the doll you are making.

KNITTING NEEDLES

The needle sizes used in this book are 2.25mm (US size 1), 3.00mm (US size 3) and 4.00mm (US size 6). The body of the work is created using 3.00mm (US size 3) needles, which produces a good fabric for the dolls' garments, but if your knitting is too tight try a size larger needles. The 2.25mm (US size 1) needles are used for detailed work.

I prefer using the short, 25cm (9¾in) length knitting needles for the small pieces of work, however some of the patterns require more stitches than can be comfortably accommodated by this length of needle. Use longer needles for working with 100 stitches or more, or if you find them more comfortable to use.

NEEDLE SIZES				
Metric:	4.00mm	3.00mm	2.75mm	2.25mm
UK (old):	no. 8	no. 11	no. 12	no. 13
US:	6	3	2	1

YARNS

The yarns used for the knitted dolls in this book are all yarns that give a similar tension range (gauge), which is 22 stitches to 10cm (4in) when used with 4.00mm (US size 6) needles and stocking stitch. Any yarn that states this tension on the ball band is therefore suitable for use with the patterns in this book. These include, in the UK, most double knitting (DK) yarns; in the USA these are known as Light Worsted and in Australia as 8 ply. These weights of yarns are widely available. Whichever yarn you choose to use, it is a good idea to use the same brand throughout the knitting of your doll as not all DK, 8 ply or Light Worsted yarns are the same.

I have used mostly acrylic yarns; compared with natural fibres, acrylic yarns tend to give more metres (or yards) to a 50g (1¾oz) ball. All the quantities of yarn given in this book are to be regarded as approximate.

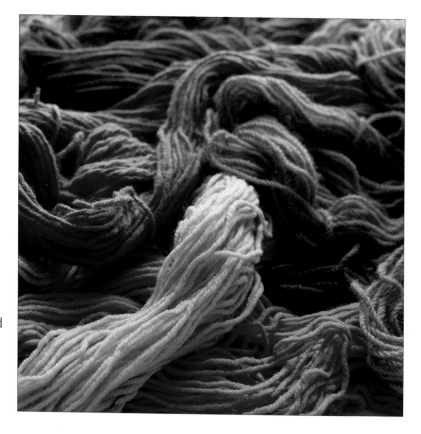

OTHER EQUIPMENT

As well as knitting needles and yarn, you will need various other pieces of equipment from time to time. These are described below.

CROCHET HOOK

You will need a 3.00mm (US size 0) crochet hook for making chain cords (see page 12).

SEWING NEEDLES

Use round-pointed tapestry needles to give good seams and stitches. A ball-pointed needle is useful for separating strands of yarn when making hair.

PINS

Always use bead-headed pins when pinning seams etc. because they are not only easy to use, but also easy to see in your work.

FILLING

Always use the best quality polyester filling that you can buy. Good filling material will spring back well when tested for firmness.

TAPE MEASURE

This is used for measuring tension swatches, and for measuring your knitting as you work.

SCISSORS

You will need a small, sharp pair of scissors for cutting the yarn.

STITCH HOLDERS

These look very much like large safety pins and are used for holding groups of stitches that are not being worked. They are available in various shapes and sizes.

ROW MARKERS

Row markers are used to mark a particular place along a row, and are easily slipped from one stitch to another. They come in various sizes and styles.

CHENILLE STICKS

For some of the dolls you will need chenille sticks (pipe cleaners). These are fibre-covered wire sticks that bend well. When you have cut the wire, turn in the end tightly as it will be rough and may cause scratching. Thicker sticks can be trimmed with scissors.

Tip

If you use a new wheel of pins at the beginning of your stitching, you will soon notice if any are missing at the end.

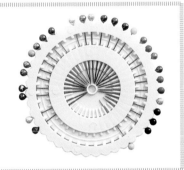

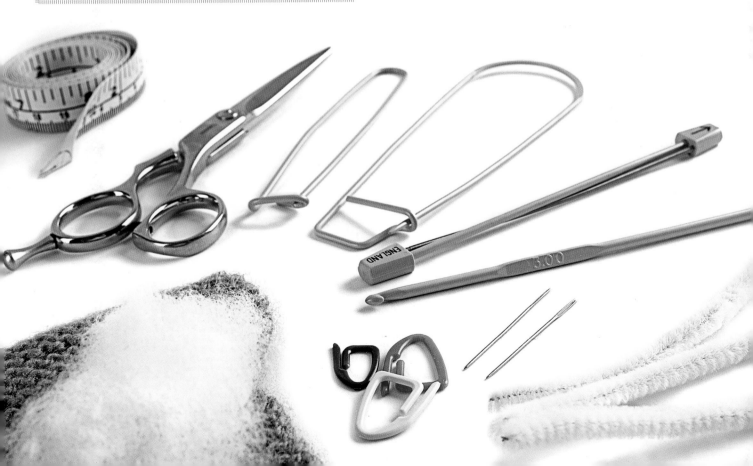

Tiny bells add an element of fun to Elizabeth Witch's stripy slippers.

Embellishments

ADDING SPARKLE

Glitter paints and glitter glue are available in many colours from most craft shops and can add a lovely sparkle to your dolls' clothes. I have used spots of gold sparkly paint on Flamenka's petals and wings, and silver on Princess Neridah's tiara. Dimensional paints can also add a little flair to your creations.

Sparkling metallic threads are just the thing to add highlights to small pieces of clothing or to make simple necklaces and bracelets. Victoria's outfit has been made just a touch more glamorous by adding shimmery, multicoloured threads here and there.

CRYSTALS, BEADS AND FAUX JEWELS

Faux jewels are available in many colours and sizes. Self-adhesive gemstones are very easy to use, and are perfect for attaching easily to your dolls' clothes and accessories. These little gems make great jewellery – stick them on to little fingers or sparkle up a hair style. They can be stuck to the bobbles on Princess Neridah's pineapple purse to add that extra piece of glamour. Crystals can be purchased by the metre and draped around the hem or collar of a cloak, for example.

Samuel Crowe has a number of beads in his hair. Search your local bead stores, markets or the internet to find some unusual beads that would suit a dashing pirate.

Find unusual beads to thread on to Samuel Crowe's hair.

Add a magic sparkle to your dolls' outfits using touches of glitter and gemstones.

APPLIQUÉ

There are all manner of braids, trims, chains and readymade items that can be applied to your dolls. Have fun searching for the right adornments to finish off your creations.

Embellishments like the readymade fabric rosebuds that I used to decorate Victoria's clothes can be purchased from craft and fabric shops and on the internet in a wide variety of colours and styles.

Just some of the materials that can be used to embellish your dolls.

Techniques

This book is intended to be enjoyed by anyone wishing to create treasured dolls. I have therefore used simple stitches that you either will already be familiar with or can learn easily from magazines, books or the internet. The stitches I have used are stocking stitch, garter stitch, rib stitch (used mainly for waistbands), moss stitch, bubble stitch (used for Princess Neridah's purse) and double loop stitch (used mainly for hair, see page 20).

Safety

When making dolls for children, safety is very important. Small items such as beads are not suitable for children under 3 years of age.

ABBREVIATIONS

Abbreviations are an integral part of all knitting patterns and the list below includes all those I have used in the book. Where an abbreviation has been created for a particular pattern, I have explained it in the relevant part of the book.

inc increase	**inc in next st** increase in the next stitch, i.e. knit into the front and then the back of the stitch	**GS** garter stitch
dec decrease		**LS** double loop stitch
K knit		**TLS** triple loop stitch
P purl	**mm** millimetre	**psso** pass slip stitch over
K2tog knit two stitches together	**cm** centimetre	**sl** slip stitch
K2tog tbl knit two stitches together to the back of the loops	**st(s)** stitch(es)	**RHS** right-hand side
	yrn yarn round needle	**LHS** left-hand side
P2tog purl two stitches together	**yon** yarn over needle	**WS** wrong side(s)
Kfb knit into the front and then the back of the stitch	**ytb** put yarn to back of work	**RS** right side(s)
	yfwd bring yarn forward	**alt** alternate
	SS stocking stitch	**dpn** double-pointed needle

TENSION

Tension is not as critical when knitting dolls as opposed to garments that are designed to be worn as most of the items are so small. There is a good tolerance allowed in the designs in this book, however a tension swatch is still recommended because not all yarns or yarn colours guarantee a good weight match (see page 8).

CORDS

I have used different styles of cord for various purposes throughout the book, including twisted yarn cords, chain cords and I-cords.

TWISTED YARN AND CHAIN CORDS

To make a 30cm (11¾in) twisted yarn cord you will need approximately 70cm (27½in) of yarn. Anchor one end and twist the yarn tightly so that when you fold the cord in half it twists firmly around itself. Knot the loose ends together. A chain cord is formed by simply crocheting single chains to the length required.

I-cord

Chain cord

Twisted yarn cord

I-CORDS
To make an I-cord you will need two double-pointed needles. Cast on two stitches (or more for a thicker cord) and knit a row. With the right side facing you, push the stitches up the needle to your right and put the needle into your left hand. The yarn is at the back and on the last stitch. Knit the stitches again. Continue in this fashion until the required length is reached.

EMBROIDERY
In most cases where I have used surface embroidery, the stitches are placed fairly randomly. Refer to the photographs that accompany the patterns for guidance. The most common embroidery stitches I have used are simple satin stitch and back stitch (used mainly on the dolls' faces; satin stitch is also used on the buttonholes on Sam Crowe's jacket), bullion knots and chain stitches (used for the rosebuds on Princess Neridah's costume), and French knots (used for the buttons on Sam Crowe's jacket). The wizard also has very simply embroidered stars and moons on his garments, which are explained in the pattern.

DUPLICATE STITCH
This stitch is used to create patterns that copy the V-shaped stocking stitches already in place. Thread a needle with a colour of your choice and bring it through to the front of the work at the base of a stocking stitch. Take the yarn across parallel with the right side of the stocking stitch and down through the work at the top of the V. Come across the back of the work and bring the needle up through on the other side of the V. Take the yarn down parallel with the left side of the stocking stitch and through to the back at the point you started from. Repeat until the motif is finished. Sew in any loose ends neatly to the back of the work, at the point from which you started.

MAKING UP
Use round, pointed tapestry needles for stitching the pieces together as these will give good seams and stitches. Use the cast-on and cast-off waste yarn wherever possible to avoid having to sew in too many loose ends.

MATTRESS STITCH
Mattress stitch, often called the hidden or invisible seam, is used to join two pieces of knitting together where both edges have an equal number of stitches. Start a half or a whole stitch in from the edge of your work, with the right sides of the work facing you (see opposite). Bring the needle up from the back on one piece of knitting, pick up two stitch loops on the other piece, then pick up two stitch loops on the first piece. Work a centimetre (half an inch) or so and pull the yarn gently to close the seam. Continue along the seam, matching the rows. Finish by sewing in the loose ends.

Seams can also be joined using back stitch and/or oversewing. Choose back stitch when sewing sleeves into armholes, and oversewing when stitching the edges of shoes and hat seams, or where flat seams are needed.

AND FINALLY...
Now all that you need to do is to sprinkle your needles with fairy dust and watch your enchanting character materialise.

Tip
To familiarise yourself with the dolls and their garments, read the patterns through first, before starting to knit.

Duplicate stitch was used to embroider the pretty hearts on Breanna's undergarments (see page 40).

Mattress stitch.

Basic body

Each doll has the same basic body, for which you will need the materials and equipment listed below. The finished height of the basic doll is approximately 45cm (18in). Begin the doll at the feet and work upwards, finishing with the head.

Materials and equipment

Needles: one pair of 3.00mm (US 3) and one pair of 2.25mm (US 1)

Approx. 100g (3½oz) double knitting (light worsted/8ply) in light beige or any flesh colour of your choice

Filling: the best quality filling that you can buy

Foot templates: cut from rigid card or plastic

Stitch holders

FEET

Begin by copying the foot templates and use them to cut out two foot shapes from either rigid card or plastic. The knitted feet are identical, but the soles (the card/plastic shapes) and filling form them into one right foot and one left foot.

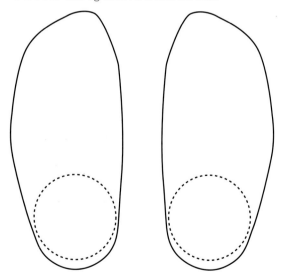

Make two feet.

For each foot:
Using 2.25mm (US 1) needles, cast on 6 sts.
row 1: inc in each st [12 sts].
row 2: purl.
row 3: inc in first and every other st, to last st, K1 [18 sts].
rows 4–18: commencing with a purl row, SS for 15 rows.

SHAPE THE TOE LINE

row 19: K2tog, K14, K2tog tbl [16 sts].
row 20: P2tog, P12, P2tog [14 sts].
row 21: K2tog, K10, K2tog tbl [12 sts].
row 22: P2tog, P8, P2tog [10 sts].
row 23: cast off 2 sts, knit to end [8 sts].
row 24: cast off 2 sts purlwise, purl to end [6 sts].
Cast off remaining sts.

MAKING UP

1. Gather around the cast-on stitches, draw the yarn up tightly and fasten.
2. Sew the edges together up to the little toe position (see template).
3. Slide in the cut-out foot shape, matching the shape of the toes.
4. Stuff moderately to give shape to the ankle and foot. Remember to stuff one to shape a left foot and the other for a right foot.
5. Oversew the remaining toe section.
6. Put aside until you are ready to sew the feet to the legs.

LEGS

The legs can be shaped to give a more mature look to the doll, or they can be left unshaped for a younger appearance.

Make two legs.

UNSHAPED LEGS

Using 3.00mm (US 3) needles, cast on 16 sts.
rows 1–62: commencing with a knit row (RS row), SS for 62 rows.

SHAPED LEGS

Using 3.00mm (US 3) needles, cast on 10 sts.
rows 1–6: commencing with a knit row, SS for 6 rows.
row 7: inc in first st, K4, inc in next st, knit to end [12 sts].
rows 8–18: commencing with a purl row, SS for 11 rows.
row 19: inc in first st, K5, inc in next st, knit to end [14 sts].
rows 20–30: commencing with a purl row, SS for 11 rows.
row 31: inc in first st, K6, inc in next st, knit to end [16 sts].
rows 32–62: commencing with a purl row, SS for 31 rows.

SHAPED AND UNSHAPED LEGS (ROW 63 ONWARDS)

Break the yarn and put the stitches of the first leg on to a stitch holder. Knit the second leg to row 62, then transfer the stitches to the RH needle. Replace the stitches from the stitch holder to the LH needle, then return the transferred stitches back from the RH to the LH needle. Work both legs with right sides facing, keeping the tension firm at the centre join of the legs.

Shape the inside thigh

row 63: inc in first st, K14, inc in next 2 sts, K14, inc in last st [36 sts].
row 64: inc in first st, P16, inc in next 2 sts, P16, inc in last st [40 sts].
row 65: inc in first st, K18, inc in next 2 sts, K18, inc in last st [44 sts].
row 66: P2tog, P18, (P2tog) twice, P18, P2tog [40 sts].
row 67: K2tog, K16, K2tog tbl, K2tog, K16, K2tog tbl [36 sts].
row 68: P2tog, P14, (P2tog) twice, P14, P2tog [32 sts].

BODY

rows 69–114: commencing with a knit row, SS for 46 rows. Mark each end of the 23rd row to indicate the waistline.

SHOULDER INDICATORS

row 115: K8, K2tog, K12, K2tog tbl, K8 [30 sts].
The shoulder indicators are the two places where you have knitted two stitches together. The arms are attached to the side of these marks.
rows 116–120: commencing with a purl row, SS for 5 rows. Mark each end of the last row to indicate the neckline.

HEAD

Change to 2.25mm (US 1) needles.
row 121: K1, (inc in next st, K1) 14 times, K1 [44 sts].
rows 122–146: commencing with a purl row, SS for 25 rows.
row 147: K1, (K2tog, K1) to last st, K1 [30 sts].
row 148: purl.
row 149: K1, (K2tog) to last st, K1 [16 sts].
row 150: purl.
row 151: (K2tog) to end of row [8 sts].
Break yarn and thread through remaining 8 sts. Finish off tightly.

MAKING UP AND FILLING

When making up and filling, the head should measure approximately 23cm (9in) round, and the chest and hips both approximately 20cm (7¾in) round.

Tip

If you are making a long-haired wig for your doll, a more solid neck is required to avoid the weight of the extra yarn pulling the head back. Make your hair piece before sewing in the loose ends. Try it for weight. If it is all right, sew in the loose ends. If not, undo the threaded yarn for the neck and re-do it less tightly, giving the doll a wider neckline to support the wig.

1. Sew the back seam of the head and half way down the back of the doll's body. Fill the head firmly, then fill part of the body. The head needs to be nicely rounded.
2. Make the neck by threading a double yarn through the row at the base of the head. Start and finish at the back of the neck. Pull the yarn firmly and knot.
3. Sew up each leg and 2cm (¾in) of the back. Fill the legs.
4. Continue to fill the body and sew up the remainder of the back.
5. Pin the ankle of the left leg to the left foot using the template as a guide. Sew through each cast-on stitch, attaching the leg to the foot neatly. Repeat for the right leg.
6. Sew in the loose ends.
7. Make a waistline by threading a double yarn through the waistline stitches as marked. Tighten to the desired waistline. Knot and sew in the loose ends.

HANDS

These playful little hands are knitted sideways and the fingers are shaped during the making-up stage. The hands are so tiny that you may need to make a few of them before you are happy with the result. The time spent doing this will be worthwhile. Each hand takes approximately 20 minutes to knit.

The knit side is the right side of the work. After each cast off, the stitch on the RH needle is not included in the next knit or purl instruction. Leave long ends (70cm; 27½in) at cast on and cast off to use when making up. This will minimise the sewing in of loose ends.

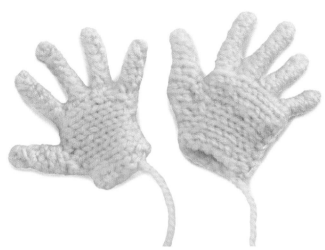

RIGHT HAND

Using 2.25 mm (US 1) needles, cast on 8 sts.
rows 1–10: commencing with a purl row, SS for 10 rows.
row 11: cast off 2 sts purlwise, P2, ytb, sl1, turn [6 sts].
row 12: ytb, sl1, knit to end.
row 13: cast on 2 sts, P4, ytb, sl1, turn [8 sts].
row 14: ytb, sl1, knit to end.
row 15: cast on 3 sts, purl to end [11 sts].
row 16: knit.
row 17: cast off 3 sts purlwise, P3, ytb, sl1, turn [8 sts].
row 18: ytb, sl1, knit to end.
row 19: cast off 2 sts purlwise, purl to end [6 sts].
row 20: knit.
row 21: cast on 8 sts, P9, ytb, sl1, turn [14 sts].
row 22: ytb, sl1, knit to end.
row 23: cast off 6 sts purlwise, purl to end [8 sts].
row 24: knit.
row 25: cast on 7 sts, P8, ytb, sl1, turn [15 sts].
row 26: ytb, sl1, knit to end.
row 27: cast off 7 sts purlwise, purl to end [8 sts].
row 28: knit.
row 29: cast on 5 sts, P7, ytb, sl1, turn [13 sts].
row 30: ytb, sl1, knit to end.
row 31: cast off 5 sts purlwise, purl to end [8 sts].
row 32: knit.
row 33: cast on 4 sts, P6, ytb, sl1, turn [12 sts].
row 34: ytb, sl1, knit to end.
Cast off purlwise loosely. (If you are a tight knitter, use a larger needle.)

LEFT HAND

Using 2.25 mm (US 1) needles, cast on 8 sts.
rows 1–10: commencing with a knit row (RS row), SS for 10 rows.
row 11: cast off 2 sts, K1, yfwd, sl1, turn [6 sts].
row 12: yfwd, sl1, purl to end.
row 13: cast on 2 sts, K5, yfwd, sl1, turn [8 sts].
row 14: yfwd, sl1, purl to end.
row 15: cast on 3 sts, knit to end [11 sts].
row 16: purl.

row 17: cast off 3 sts, K3, yfwd, sl1, turn [8 sts].
row 18: yfwd, sl1, purl to end.
row 19: cast off 2 sts, knit to end [6 sts].
row 20: purl.
row 21: cast on 8 sts, K9, yfwd, sl1, turn [14 sts].
row 22: yfwd, sl1, purl to end.
row 23: cast off 6 sts, knit to end [8 sts].
row 24: purl.
row 25: cast on 7 sts, K8, yfwd, sl1, turn [15 sts].
row 26: yfwd, sl1, purl to end.
row 27: cast off 7 sts, knit to end [8 sts].
row 28: purl.
row 29: cast on 5 sts, K7, yfwd, sl1, turn [13 sts].
row 30: yfwd, sl1, purl to end.
row 31: cast off 5 sts, knit to end [8 sts].
row 32: purl.
row 33: cast on 4 sts, K6, yfwd, sl1, turn [12 sts].
row 34: yfwd, sl1, purl to end.
Cast off loosely. (If you are a tight knitter, use a larger needle.)

MAKING UP THE HANDS

Read the instructions through first. Start sewing up the fingers at the base of the little finger.

1. Using the waste yarn from the cast-off stitches, weave the cast-off yarn through to the base of the little finger and make an anchor stitch.
2. With your left thumb and index finger, pinch the finger edges together (purl side inside). Pick up the outer stitch either side of the finger and pull the cast-on and cast-off edges into the centre of the finger, making a neat seam.
3. After sewing up the finger, take the needle down the centre of the finger back to the base. Pull the yarn sufficiently to make a firm, straight finger. Put an anchor stitch at the base between the little finger and the next finger.
4. Continue along each finger then the thumb. Finally, sew the top edge of the palm to the base of the fingers and join up the side of the hand. Sometimes a little practice is needed here.
5. Fill the palm slightly.
6. With the cast-on waste yarn, make gathering stitches around the wrist edge.
7. Attach the thumb pad to the palm under the first finger by pinching the base of the thumb into the palm and oversewing with three stitches to hold it in place.

Put the hands aside until you are ready to attach them to the arms.

ARMS

Shape the arms to give a more mature look to the dolls, or leave them unshaped for a younger appearance.

Make two arms.

UNSHAPED ARMS

Start with the wrist line.
Using 3.00mm (US 3) needles, cast on 12 sts.
rows 1–44: SS for 44 rows.

SHAPED ARMS

Start with the wrist line.
Using 3.00mm (US 3) needles, cast on 8 sts.
rows 1–6: SS for 6 rows.
row 7: K1, inc in next st, K2, inc in next st, K3 [10 sts].
rows 8–28: commencing with a purl row, SS for 21 rows.
row 29: K1, inc in next st, K3, inc in next st, K4 [12 sts].
rows 30–44: commencing with a purl row, SS for 15 rows.

SHAPED AND UNSHAPED ARMS (ROW 45 ONWARDS)

row 45: K2tog, K8, K2tog tbl [10 sts].
row 46: P2tog, P6, P2tog [8 sts].
row 47: K2tog, K4, K2tog tbl [6 sts].
row 48: P2tog, P2, P2tog [4 sts].
Cast off remaining sts.

MAKING UP THE ARMS

1. Gather up the cast-on edge and finish tightly.
2. Sew the row ends together up to the shoulder decreases.
3. Stuff the arms firmly with filling.

ATTACHING THE HANDS TO THE ARMS

1. Push the wrist edge of the arm into the wrist edge of the hand, keeping the seam of the arm aligned with the centre of the palm. Pin it in place if needed. Tighten the gathered stitching. Sew in place.
2. Check the fingers for straightness. If further sculpting is required, push the needle up and down the centre of each finger to add stiffness and adjust the shape of the finger.

ATTACHING THE ARMS TO THE BODY

1. Pin the arms to the body, so that the seams are on the inside, facing the body. Place them just to the side of the shoulder indicators (see page 16).
2. Sew the arms to the body.

Making faces

Putting on the face is an exciting part of your doll's creation. This is the stage at which you give your doll its special character, using different coloured yarns and lengths of stitch to give your doll its own eyes, mouth and eyebrows. Instructions for making the dolls' faces are given with the patterns for the individual dolls, however there are some general guidelines that should be followed.

It is easier to create your doll's face before sewing on the hair piece (see pages 20–21). Start the stitching by passing the needle through from the back of the head, and once the stitching is completed return the needle to the back of the head to finish off. Check the appearance of your doll continually as you work, and don't sew in the loose ends until you are entirely happy with the features you have made. To finish, add a little red crayon or chalk to the cheeks to give them a slight blush.

EYES

Eyes are usually stitched using black yarn. Keep them at least three full knitting stitches apart, with the centre of the eye approximately 16 rows up from the neck. They should be 8–14mm (½–¾in) in diameter, though you may decide to make them a little bigger or smaller than this, or even to place one higher than the other. Experiment to give the best look for your particular doll's face.

The eyes are created using several (usually 8–10) satin stitches. Vary the length of the stitches to suit the size of the eye that you wish to create. Highlight the eye with four white stitches placed in a wedge shape in the top right-hand corner. To add eye colour, work a line of short back stitches around the top of the eye and out towards where the ears would be.

If eyebrows are needed, use yarn in the same colour as the hair and put in one or two single strands above each eye. Daisy Livingstone Fairy has antennae, like a butterfly, instead of eyebrows. Make them out of short lengths of chain cord or twisted cord (see page 12). Pass one end through, above the centre of the eye, and finish off at the back of the head, leaving the other end free.

MOUTH

The mouth stitching should be placed about nine rows up from the neck and centred on the face. Various shades of pink, red, orange or plum yarn can be used. Vary the shape of the mouth by lengthening or shortening the stitches, or by altering the number of stitches used.

Tip

You might find it helpful to sketch out your doll's face on paper before stitching, to make sure you are happy with the shapes, colours and positioning of the features. Have fun creating faces with different characters and expressions!

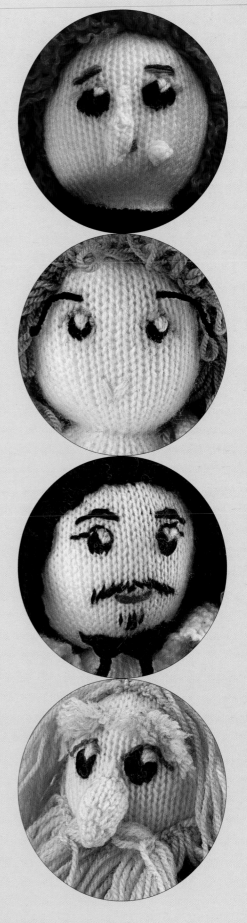

Hair pieces

The hair pieces are little wigs that start at the nape of the neck, increase and decrease in width following the shape of the head, and finish at the forehead. To attach the hair piece to your doll's head, gather the stitches around the edge of the wig, settle it nicely on to the doll's head and then pin it into position before stitching firmly in place. If required, sew in plaited extensions, dreadlocks or beaded lengths of hair that you have made separately. To fluff the hair, separate each strand of yarn with a ball-pointed needle. This takes a little time but is very effective.

The stitches used for the hair pieces are garter stitch and double loop stitch (LS). The loops can be made any length and either left as loops, giving the effect of soft curls, or cut for straight hair. Cutting the loops unevenly can also give an interesting hair style. A single row of loop stitches made separately can be added for a fringe, and this stitch can also used for eyebrows and beards. For a thicker look, use triple loop stitch.

If you are using a two-fingered loop stitch (see page 21) you will need approximately 60g (2oz) of yarn in a colour of your choice. For very long hair you will need more than this, though you can reduce the amount used by knitting rows 5, 11 and 15 rather than using loop stitch.

Work commences at the nape of the neck.
Using 3.00mm (US 3) needles, cast on 16 sts.
row 1: LS to end of row.
row 2: K1, inc in next st, K12, inc in next st, K1 [18 sts].
row 3: LS to end of row.
row 4: K1, inc in next st, K14, inc in next st, K1 [20 sts].
row 5: LS to end of row.
row 6: K1, inc in next st, K16, inc in next st, K1 [22 sts].
row 7: LS to end of row.
row 8: for shaping the crown of the wig, complete the following instructions from * to * using the first of the two figures in the brackets: *K(16, 19), sl1, turn, ytb, sl1, K(10, 14), sl1, turn, ytb, sl1, K(8, 12), sl1, turn, ytb, sl1, LS (6, 9), sl1, turn, ytb, sl1, knit to end of row.*
row 9: LS to end of row.
row 10: K1, inc in next st, K18, inc in next st, K1 [24 sts].
row 11: LS to end of row.
row 12: knit.
row 13: LS to end of row.
row 14: complete the instructions for row 8 from * to * using the second of the two figures in the brackets.
row 15: LS to end of row.
row 16: knit.
row 17: LS to end of row.
row 18: knit.
row 19: LS4, K16, LS4.

row 20: complete the instructions for row 8 from * to * using the second of the two figures in the brackets.
row 21: LS8, K8, LS8.
row 22: K1, K2tog, K18, K2tog tbl, K1 [22 sts].
row 23: LS4, K14, LS4.
row 24: K1, K2tog, K16, K2tog tbl, K1 [20 sts].
row 25: LS to end of row.
row 26: K1, K2tog, K14, K2tog tbl, K1 [18 sts].
row 27: LS4, K10, LS4.
row 28: K1, (K2tog) twice, K8, (K2tog tbl) twice, K1 [14 sts].
row 29: LS to end of row.
row 30: K1, (K2tog) twice, K4, (K2tog tbl) twice, K1 [10 sts].
row 31: LS to end of row.
row 32: K2tog to end of row [5 sts].
row 33: LS2, *pass first knitted stitch over second stitch, LS1*, repeat from * to * to end of row.
Cast off, leaving a long length of waste yarn.

FINISHING OFF

With the waste yarn, put a gathering stitch around the edge of the hair piece. Fit the wig to the doll's head and pin it in place, easing it into position where necessary. Pull the gathering yarn up to fit the hair comfortably to the head. Sew the wig firmly in place. If using a fringe, place the hair piece a little further back on the head to allow for the width of the fringe at the front.

BASIC FRINGE

Use triple loop stitch (TLS) or double loop stitch (LS).

Using 3.00mm (US 3) needles, cast on 20 sts.
row 1: TLS (or LS) to the end of the row.
Cast off here for a single fringe. If a thicker fringe is required, continue with rows 2 and 3.
row 2: K1, inc in next st, K16, inc in next st, K1 [22 sts].
row 3: TLS (or LS) to the end of the row.
Cast off.

Pinch the cast-off and cast-on rows together and oversew to make a narrow edge to the fringe. Pin the fringe to the forehead, close to the edge of the hair piece. Keep the loops forward. Sew the fringe in place. Cut and style the fringe as you wish.

DOUBLE LOOP STITCH (LS)

When knitting the loop stitch, wrap the yarn around one, two or more fingers to get the length of hair (size of loop) that you require. Remember to pull each loop stitch firmly as you work along the row to secure the stitches.

1. Cast on the required number of stitches.
2. Put the RH needle into the first stitch on the LH needle as if you are going to knit a stitch, then put the yarn around the needle.
3. Put the yarn around the needle again but this time make a loop with the yarn by putting it around one or more fingers of the left hand as well.
4. Pull the two strands through on to the RH needle. Transfer the two strands back on to the LH needle and knit the two stitches together.
5. Pull the loop made at the back (right side of the work) to tighten the stitch and make it firm. When the wig is complete the loops can be cut to make separate strands of hair.

TRIPLE LOOP STITCH (TLS)

For a fuller fringe, eyebrows or a very full wig, knit a triple loop stitch with an extra loop, that is, having three strands of yarn over the needles. Pull the three strands through as in ordinary knit stitch. Transfer the stitches to the LH needle and knit all three stitches together. This gives two loops to the stitch instead of just one. Remember to pull the loops to secure the stitch.

Elizabeth Witch's hair piece (shown in the centre on page 20) and fringe could also be knitted in multicoloured yarn.

Elizabeth Witch

Elizabeth Witch wears a warm undertop and pants with secret pockets, one of which she uses for her wishes. Her long-sleeved blouse has a collar that is V-shaped at the back and the front, and both of Elizabeth's skirts, the top skirt and the underskirt, are shaped to flare at the bottom and are long enough to keep her warm in the winter. I am a little surprised that her skirts are flared, and the top skirt has a pleated effect, because Elizabeth is usually very traditional in her choice of witchery clothing, but I do believe she likes the way her skirt swings as she walks and I did catch her once doing a twirl after she had made a very special spell! On her hands she wears a pair of fingerless mittens and on her head is perched a splendidly pointed hat, complete with hat band.

The shoes Elizabeth wears during the day are typically smart and practical, but she also has a pair of cosy pointed slippers which she wears on cold nights when she is sitting in front of her lovely warm log fire. She drapes her shawl over her shoulders to keep the draughts at bay, or wraps it around her waist in case she needs it whilst she is out shopping.

When Elizabeth goes out searching for herbs she takes her satchel with her, which she fills with many mystical things. Sometimes she also takes her broomstick.

Begin by knitting the basic body for your doll (see pages 14–18).

Materials and equipment

Needles: one pair each of: 4.00mm (US 6), 3.00mm (US 3) and 2.25mm (US 1)

Crochet hook: 3.00mm (US 0)

Stitch holders

Black and white chenille sticks for the broomstick and wand

Tiny bells to decorate slippers (optional)

Needle with eye large enough for yarn, e.g. tapestry needle

Bead-headed pins

Filling: the best quality polyester filling that you can buy

Yarns (approximate amounts):
100g (3½oz) cream/flesh coloured for basic body
60g (2oz) auburn shades for hair
300g (10½oz) black for clothes and accessories
50g (1¾oz) purple for pants, vest and eye shading
small amounts of white, yellow, lime green, black and pink for details and face

FACE

Embroider the eyes and mouth following the general guidelines given on page 19. Use the photograph below for guidance, but feel free to use your imagination to create a character of your own.

HOOKED NOSE

Commence knitting at the top of the nose and finish at the tip (row 13).

Using 2.25mm (US 1) needles and a small amount of the flesh-coloured yarn, cast on 2 sts.

row 1: inc in each st [4 sts].
row 2: purl.
row 3: inc in first and third sts [6 sts].
rows 4–6: commencing with a knit row, SS for 3 rows.
row 7: K2, inc in next 2 sts, K2 [8 sts].
row 8: purl.
row 9: K2tog, K1, K2tog tbl, K1, K2tog tbl [5 sts].
row 10: purl.
row 11: K2tog, K1, K2tog tbl [3 sts].
row 12: purl.
row 13: K1, sl1, psso, put RH stitch on to LH needle, pull left stitch over right stitch.

Break yarn, leaving enough yarn for sewing.

FINISHING OFF

1. Oversew the edges of the nose from the tip upwards. Fill it slightly as you go. Sew up the remainder of the seam.
2. Sew the top half of the nose to Elizabeth's face with the top of the nose placed centrally and aligned with the middle of her eyes.

WART

Using 2.25mm (US 1) needles and a small amount of the flesh-coloured yarn, cast on 6 sts.
Cast off.

Sew gathering stitches around the edges of the knitting and draw them together into a small ball. Flatten and sew the wart to Elizabeth's chin.

To add some facial hair, sew a strand of yarn into the wart and leave the end free. Separate the strand into fine pieces and cut them to different lengths.

HAIR

1. Using the auburn-coloured yarn, follow the pattern for the basic hair piece (pages 20–21), but make the loops by winding the yarn around four fingers loosely or two fingers twice, whichever is the more comfortable for you. Cut through the loops to make straight hair and attach the hair piece to the witch's head.
2. Make the fringe with two-finger triple loop stitch. Again, cut through each loop and attach it to the front of Elizabeth's head. Trim the fringe to the shape of the face.
3. Trim the hair piece a little at the front to match the fringe so that the seam is covered as much as possible.

Tip

Cut the loops unevenly so that there are long and short sections of hair. This gives it a dishevelled look (I do believe that most witches are probably a little forgetful about combing their hair).

4. Fluff up the hair by separating the strands in the yarn using a ball-pointed needle.

5. Make two little plaits each 20cm (7¾in) long using three strands of hair-coloured yarn. Knot the ends of the plait, leaving about 1cm (½in) of yarn after each knot, and fluff up the loose ends.

6. Thread a plait through the hair piece on either side of the head just above eye level. Make one plait a little longer than the other and secure them to the hair piece with a couple of stitches using hair-coloured yarn.

LONG-SLEEVED BLOUSE

FRONT AND BACK

Using 3.00mm (US 3) needles, cast on 37 sts loosely. (If you tend to knit tightly, use a larger needle.)
row 1: knit.
row 2: purl.
row 3: knit.
row 4: knit (hem edge).
row 5: K1, (K5, P1) 5 times, K6.
row 6: K1, (P5, K1) 6 times.
rows 7–12: repeat rows 5 and 6, 3 times.
row 13: K1, (K2tog, K3, P1) 5 times, K2tog, K3, K1 [31 sts].
row 14: K1, (P4, K1) 6 times.
row 15: K1, (K4, P1) 5 times, K5.
rows 16–25: repeat rows 14 and 15, 5 times.
row 26: repeat row 14.

Armhole shaping

row 27: cast off 3 sts, (with 1 st on needle) K1, (P1, K4) 5 times, K1 [28 sts].
row 28: cast off 3 sts, (with 1 st on needle) P1, (K1, P4) 4 times, K1, P1, K1 [25 sts].
row 29: K2, (P1, K4) 4 times, P1, K2.
row 30: K1, P1, (K1, P4) 4 times, K1, P1, K1.
rows 31–36: repeat rows 29 and 30, 3 times.

Shaping left-hand side of neckline

row 37: K2, P1, K4, P1, K1, yfwd, sl1, turn, yfwd, sl1, P1, K1, P4, K1, P1, K1.
row 38: K2, P1, K4, yfwd, sl1, turn, yfwd, sl1, P4, K1, P1, K1.
row 39: K2, P1, K2, yfwd, sl1, turn, yfwd, sl1, P2, K1, P1, K1.
row 40: cast off 4 sts, (with 1 st on needle) K2, (P1, K4) 3 times, P1, K2 [21 sts].

Shaping right-hand side of neckline

row 41: K1, P1, K1, P4, K1, P1, ytb, sl1, turn, ytb, sl1, K1, P1, K4, P1, K2.
row 42: K1, P1, K1, P4, ytb, sl1, turn, ytb, sl1, K4, P1, K2.
row 43: K1, P1, K1, P2, ytb, sl1, turn, ytb, sl1, K2, P1, K2.
row 44: (WS row) cast off 4 sts, (with 1 st on needle) P2, (K1, P4) twice, K1, P2, K1 [17 sts].

Shaping the collar

For this part, the right and wrong sides of the knitting are reversed so that the right side of the collar is visible when folded over the outside of the blouse.

For the collar fold line:
row 45: cast on 6 sts, knit to end [23 sts].
row 46: cast on 6 sts, knit to end [29 sts].

Shaping the neckline of the collar

row 47: K6, P1, ytb, sl1, turn, ytb, sl1, K7, K6, P3, ytb, sl1, turn, ytb, sl1, K9, K6, P5, ytb, sl1, turn, ytb, sl1, K11, K6, purl to last 6 sts, K6.
row 48: K7, yfwd, sl1, turn, yfwd, sl1, P1, K6, K9, yfwd, sl1, turn, yfwd, sl1, P3, K6, K11, yfwd, sl1, turn, yfwd, sl1, P5, K6.

Long-sleeved blouse, front and back, shown here in a different colour so that the stitching shows up clearly.

decrease pattern A (dpA): slip second st on LH needle over the first st, then knit the first st.

row 49: K6, sl1, K1, psso, K13, dpA, K6 [27 sts].
row 50: K6, P15, K6.
row 51: K6, sl1, K1, psso, K11, dpA, K6 [25 sts].
row 52: K6, P13, K6.
row 53: K6, sl1, K1, psso, K9, dpA, K6 [23 sts].
row 54: K6, P11, K6.
row 55: K6, sl1, K1, psso, K7, dpA, K6 [21 sts].
row 56: K6, P9, K6.
row 57: K6, sl1, K1, psso, K5, dpA, K6 [19 sts].
row 58: K6, P7, K6.
row 59: K6, sl1, K1, psso, K3, dpA, K6 [17 sts].
row 60: K6, P5, K6.
row 61: K6, sl1, K1, psso, K1, dpA, K6 [15 sts].
row 62: K6, P3, K6.

decrease pattern B (dpB): slip the st just knitted back on to the LH needle, slip second st on that needle over the first st. Slip that st back on to the RH needle.

row 63: K6, sl1, K1, psso, dpB, K6 [13 sts].
row 64: K6, P1, K6.
row 65: K5, sl1, K1, psso, dpB, K5 [11 sts].
row 66: K5, P1, K5.
row 67: K4, sl1, K1, psso, dpB, K4 [9 sts].
row 68: K4, P1, K4.
row 69: K3, sl1, K1, psso, dpB, K3 [7 sts].
row 70: K3, P1, K3.
row 71: K2, sl1, K1, psso, dpB, K2 [5 sts].
row 72: K2, P1, K2.
row 73: K1, sl1, K1, psso, dpB, K1 [3 sts].
row 74: K1, P1, K1.
row 75: sl1, K1, psso, dpB [1 st].
Pass yarn through remaining st. Sew in the loose ends.

SLEEVES

Make two sleeves.

Cast on 26 sts loosely (or use a larger needle).
row 1: knit.
row 2: purl.
row 3: knit.
row 4: knit (cuff edge).
row 5: K5, (P1, K4) 4 times, K1.
row 6: K1, (P4, K1) 5 times.
rows 7–40: repeat rows 5 and 6, 17 times.
Cast off loosely.
Sew up the edges of the sleeve and cuff, keeping the right sides to the outside. Turn the cuff under and sew the hem. This hem gives a little bell shape to the end of the sleeves, which matches the blouse and skirt hemlines.

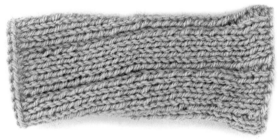

A completed sleeve, shown in a different colour so that the stitching shows up clearly.

MAKING UP

Sew up the sides and shoulders of the blouse. Turn the blouse inside-out and, keeping the sleeves right side out, tuck the top edge of each sleeve into the armholes from inside the blouse (RS facing). Match the sleeve seams with the side seams of the blouse. Pin the sleeves then stitch them in place. Turn under the hem of the blouse.

The completed long-sleeved blouse.

Change to 2.25 mm (US 1) needles.
row 59: (K1, P1) to end.
row 60: repeat row 59.
row 61: K1, (yrn, K2tog) to last st, yrn, K1.
row 62: (K1, P1) to last st, K1.
Cast off ribwise.

MAKING UP

Sew in any loose ends. Sew each leg seam (inside leg). Sew the body front and back seams together, leaving 4cm (1½in) of the back seam free below the waistline to allow easier fitting. Make a 40cm (15¾in) cord (see page 12) and thread it through the waistline.

POCKETS

Make five pockets in various sizes.
Cast on 8 or 10 sts.
SS for 8–16 rows.
Moss stitch for 3 rows.
Cast off in pattern.
Pin and sew the pockets to the pants in various positions.

Tip

Elizabeth uses her pockets for storing secret spells and wishes. Put her wand in one pocket (see page 34), and write a wish on a tiny piece of paper and place it in another pocket, along with some sparkly glitter for an extra magical touch.

UNDERSKIRT

Using 3.00mm (US 3) needles, cast on 160 sts loosely.
rows 1–5: SS, commencing with a knit row.
row 6: K2, (yrn, K2tog) to last 2 sts, K2 (this is the picot hemline).

Change to 4.00mm (US 6) needles.
rows 7–10: SS, commencing with a knit row.
row 11: K9, (K2tog, K18) 7 times, K2tog, K8 [152 sts].
row 12: purl.
row 13: knit.
row 14: purl.
row 15: K9, (K2tog, K17) 7 times, K2tog, K8 [144 sts].
row 16: purl.
row 17: knit.
row 18: purl.

Elizabeth's underskirt is knitted mostly on 4.00mm (US 6) needles. This gives a softer, fuller effect. Not only does Elizabeth find it lovely and warm to wear, but it also helps to shape her top skirt nicely. It is knitted in one piece. The inner part of the hem is knitted with 3.00mm (US 3) needles to help the hem lay flat.

row 19: K8, (K2tog, K16) 7 times, K2tog, K8 [136 sts].
row 20: purl.
row 21: knit.
row 22: purl.
row 23: K8, (K2tog, K15) 7 times, K2tog, K7 [128 sts].
row 24: purl.
row 25: knit.
row 26: purl.
row 27: K7, (K2tog, K14) 7 times, K2tog, K7 [120 sts].
row 28: purl.
row 29: knit.
row 30: purl.
row 31: K7, (K2tog, K13) 7 times, K2tog, K6 [112 sts].
row 32: purl.
row 33: knit.
row 34: purl.
row 35: K6, (K2tog, K12) 7 times, K2tog, K6 [104 sts].
row 36: purl.
row 37: knit.
row 38: purl.

row 39: K6, (K2tog, K11) 7 times, K2tog, K5 [96 sts].
row 40: purl.
row 41: knit.
row 42: purl.
row 43: K5, (K2tog, K10) 7 times, K2tog, K5 [88 sts].
row 44: purl.
row 45: knit.
row 46: purl.
row 47: K5, (K2tog, K9) 7 times, K2tog, K4 [80 sts].
row 48: purl.
row 49: knit.
row 50: purl.
row 51: K4, (K2tog, K8) 7 times, K2tog, K4 [72 sts].
row 52: purl.
row 53: knit.
row 54: purl.
row 55: K4, (K2tog, K7) 7 times, K2tog, K3 [64 sts].
row 56: purl.
row 57: knit.
row 58: purl.
row 59: K3, (K2tog, K6) 7 times, K2tog, K3 [56 sts].
row 60: purl.
row 61: knit.
row 62: purl.
row 63: K3, (K2tog, K5) 7 times, K2tog, K2 [48 sts].
rows 64–72: SS, commencing with a purl row.

Change to 3.00mm (US 3) needles.
rows 73–74: (K1, P1) to end of row.
row 75: K1, (yrn, K2tog) to last st, yrn, K1.
row 76: (K1, P1) to last st, K1.
Cast off ribwise.

MAKING UP

Sew the back seam, leaving a 4cm (1½in) gap below the waistline. Make a 40cm (15¾in) cord (see page 12) and thread it through the waistline starting at the centre back. Turn the hemline at the picot edge and pin in place. Sew the hemline.

SHOES

SOLE

Make two.

Knitting begins at the heel.
Using 2.25mm (US 1) needles, cast on 4 sts.
row 1: knit.
row 2: K1, inc in next 2 sts, K1 [6 sts].
rows 3–14: GS.
row 15: K1, inc in next st, K2, inc in next st, K1 [8 sts].
rows 16–30: GS.
row 31: K1, K2tog, K2, K2tog, K1 [6 sts].
row 32: knit.
row 33: K2tog, K2, K2tog tbl [4 sts].
row 34: knit.
row 35: K2tog, K2tog tbl [2 sts].
row 36: knit.
row 37: K2tog.
Sew in the loose ends.

SIDES

Make four.

Cast on 6 sts.
row 1: knit.
row 2: K1, inc 1 st in next st, K2, inc 1 st in next st, K1 [8 sts].
rows 3–14: GS.
row 15: K1, inc in next st, knit to end [9 sts].
row 16: knit to last 2 sts, inc in next st, K1 [10 sts].
rows 17–18: repeat rows 15 and 16.
row 19: repeat row 15 [13 sts].
row 20: knit.

row 21: K1, K2tog, knit to end [12 sts].
row 22: knit.
rows 23–41: repeat rows 21 and 22, 9 times [3 sts].
row 42: K1, K2tog.
row 43: knit.
row 44: K2tog.
Sew in any loose ends.

STRAP

Cast on 3 sts.
rows 1–40: GS.
row 41: K2tog, K1.
row 42: K2tog (this makes a small pointed end).
Sew the flat (not tapered) end of the strap to the inside edge of the shoe.

BUCKLE

Wrap yarn around your index finger twice and use buttonhole stitch to bind the strands together to form a circle. Sew the top and bottom of the buckle to the outer side of the shoe. Lay the strap across the shoe and thread it through the buckle.

MITTENS

Make two.

Using 2.25mm (US 1) needles, cast on 20 sts.
Rib (K1, P1) for 2 rows.
SS for 10 rows.
Cast off.
Sew the edges of the two rows of ribbing together. Leave a six-row gap for the thumb to go through and sew the remaining edges together.

The parts of each shoe, including two sides, sole, strap and buckle, shown in light blue so that the stitching is easier to see.

MAKING UP

Sew the cast-on edges of the shoe sides together. Include the first increases to give a slight curve to the heel. Sew the upper part of the shoe from the point of the toe to within 1cm (½in) of the opening. Sew the edges of the sole to the lower edges of the shoe sides, matching the toe and the heel.

WAND

Cut a white chenille stick down to length 12cm (4¾in). Pinch the ends of the wire over to make sure that there are no sharp ends.
Using 3.00mm (US 3) needles, cast on 30 sts.
SS for 6 rows.
Cast off.
Using the natural roll of the knitting, wrap the knitting lengthwise around the chenille stick. Pinch the edges together and pin in place. Oversew the edges by picking up the outside of the cast-on and cast-off stitches. Secure the top and the bottom of the wand with a few stitches.

BROOMSTICK

Cut a black chenille stick to length 30cm (11¾in).
Using 3.00mm (US 3) needles, cast on 60 sts.
SS for 6 rows.
Cast off.
Wrap the knitting (with purl side on the outside) around the chenille stick lengthwise using the natural curl of the knitting. Pinch the edges together and pin in place. Oversew the edges.

BRUSH

Make the brush by wrapping yarn around four fingers loosely about 40 times. Cut through the loops (the strands should be approximately 15cm/6in in length). Lay them down and place the broomstick handle about one-third of the way into the 'bristles'. Wrap a length of yarn very tightly around the yarn strands and the handle to hold them in place. Sew through the strands into the broom handle to secure the wrapping yarn. Trim the strands so they are not all the same length.

SATCHEL

Using 3.00mm (US 3) needles, cast on 20 sts.
rows 1–5: GS.
row 6: K4, P12, K4.
row 7: knit.
row 8: K4, P12, K4.
rows 9–20: repeat rows 7 and 8, 6 times.
rows 21–30: GS (rows 26–30 form the base of the satchel).

Block A (rows 31–34):
row 31: K4, P4, K4, P4, K4.
row 32: P4, K4, P4, K4, P4.
rows 33–34: repeat rows 31 and 32.

Block B (rows 35–38):
row 35: P4, K4, P4, K4, P4.
row 36: K4, P4, K4, P4, K4.
rows 37–38: repeat rows 35 and 36.

rows 39–62: repeat blocks A and B alternately for 5 blocks, commencing with block A.
row 63: cast off 4 sts, K4, P4, K8 [16 sts].
row 64: cast off 4 sts, P4, K4, P4 [12 sts].
row 65: K4, P4, K4.
row 66: P4, K4, P4.
row 67: cast off 4 sts, K8 [8 sts].
row 68: cast off 4 sts, P4 [4 sts].
row 69: K4.
row 70: P4.
row 71: cast off 4 sts.

With remaining st on needle, crochet 10 chain stitches using a 3.00mm (US 0) crochet hook. Break yarn and put the yarn through the last st. Sew the chain to the other corner of the last row to make a loop. Sew in the loose ends. The completed satchel (including the button), before making up, is shown opposite.

STRAP

Cast on 4 sts.
GS for 50cm (19¾in).
Cast off.
Sew the cast-on edge of the strap to the base (rows 26–30) on one side of the satchel, and the cast-off edge of the strap to the base on the other side of the satchel. To form the sides of the satchel, sew the strap up from the base on each side of the satchel to the top edge of the satchel front.

BUTTON

Cast on 5 sts.
SS for 5 rows.
Cast off.
Go with the natural roll of the knitting and sew it into a sausage shape, purl side on the outside. Sew the middle of the button on to the front of the satchel.

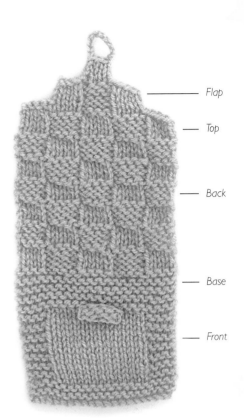

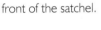

The satchel, before making up, shown in a lighter colour so that the stitching can be seen clearly.

— Flap
— Top
— Back
— Base
— Front

In her satchel, Elizabeth sometimes carries a finely knitted cloth for wrapping up her precious finds, and tiny bottles filled with sparkly spells and magic wishes.

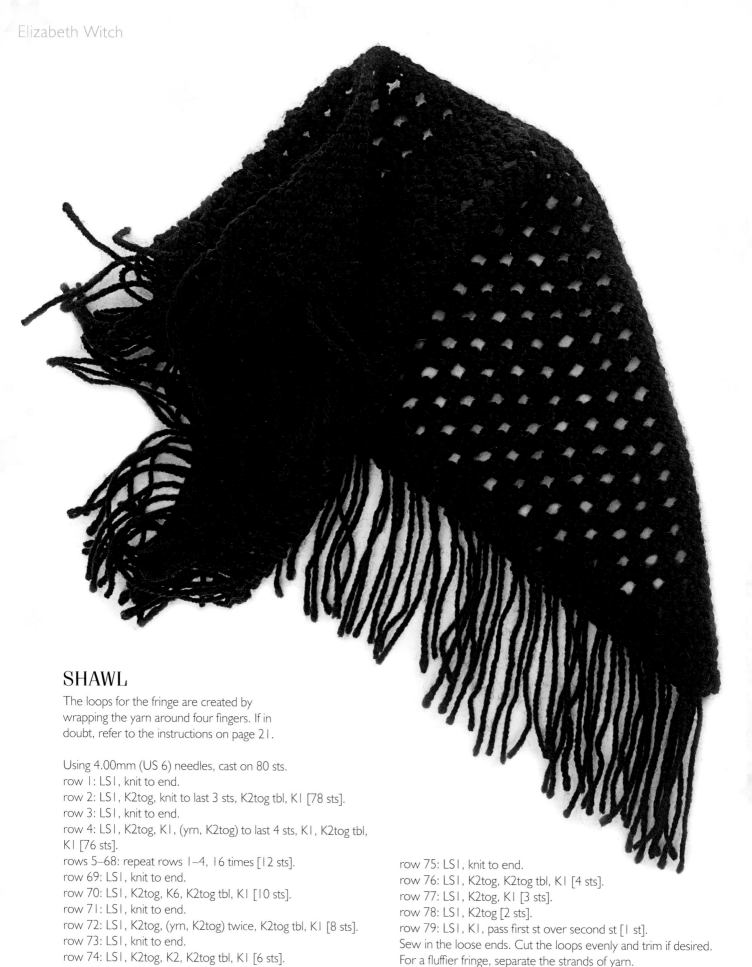

SHAWL

The loops for the fringe are created by
wrapping the yarn around four fingers. If in
doubt, refer to the instructions on page 21.

Using 4.00mm (US 6) needles, cast on 80 sts.
row 1: LS1, knit to end.
row 2: LS1, K2tog, knit to last 3 sts, K2tog tbl, K1 [78 sts].
row 3: LS1, knit to end.
row 4: LS1, K2tog, K1, (yrn, K2tog) to last 4 sts, K1, K2tog tbl,
K1 [76 sts].
rows 5–68: repeat rows 1–4, 16 times [12 sts].
row 69: LS1, knit to end.
row 70: LS1, K2tog, K6, K2tog tbl, K1 [10 sts].
row 71: LS1, knit to end.
row 72: LS1, K2tog, (yrn, K2tog) twice, K2tog tbl, K1 [8 sts].
row 73: LS1, knit to end.
row 74: LS1, K2tog, K2, K2tog tbl, K1 [6 sts].

row 75: LS1, knit to end.
row 76: LS1, K2tog, K2tog tbl, K1 [4 sts].
row 77: LS1, K2tog, K1 [3 sts].
row 78: LS1, K2tog [2 sts].
row 79: LS1, K1, pass first st over second st [1 st].
Sew in the loose ends. Cut the loops evenly and trim if desired.
For a fluffier fringe, separate the strands of yarn.

SLIPPERS

Elizabeth loves her lime green and yellow striped slippers, but she would be just as happy with two different colours of your choice. The more garish the better! And if you can find some tiny bells for the toes, I am sure Elizabeth will be delighted.

Using 3.00mm (US 3) needles, cast on 24 sts.
rows 1–4: rib (K1, P1) in colour 1 (C1).
rows 5–6: rib (K1, P1) in colour 2 (C2).
rows 7–8: SS in C1.
rows 9–10: SS in C2.
rows 11–18: repeat rows 7–10, twice.

Using C1, shape the heel.
Carry C2 up side of work, weaving with C1.
row 19: K8, sl1, turn, ytb, sl1, yfwd, P8.
row 20: K7, sl1, turn, ytb, sl1, yfwd, P7.
row 21: K6, sl1, turn, ytb, sl1, yfwd, P6.
row 22: K5, sl1, turn, ytb, sl1, yfwd, P5.
row 23: K4, sl1, turn, ytb, sl1, yfwd, P4.
row 24: K3, sl1, turn, ytb, sl1, yfwd, P3.
row 25: repeat row 23.
row 26: repeat row 22.
row 27: repeat row 21.
row 28: repeat row 20.
row 29: knit across all sts.
row 30: P8, sl1, turn, yfwd, sl1, ytb, K8.
row 31: P7, sl1, turn, yfwd, sl1, ytb, K7.

row 32: P6, sl1, turn, yfwd, sl1, ytb, K6.
row 33: P5, sl1, turn, yfwd, sl1, ytb, K5.
row 34: P4, sl1, turn, yfwd, sl1, ytb, K4.
row 35: P3, sl1, turn, yfwd, sl1, ytb, K3.
row 36: repeat row 34.
row 37: repeat row 33.
row 38: repeat row 32.
row 39: repeat row 31.
row 40: purl across all sts.
rows 41–42: SS in C2.
row 43: keeping to the two-row stripe, (K2tog, K4) 4 times [20 sts].
row 44: purl.
rows 45–46: SS.
row 47: (K2tog, K3) 4 times [16 sts].
rows 48–50: repeat rows 44–46.
row 51: (K2tog, K2) 4 times [12 sts].
rows 52–54: repeat rows 44–46.
row 55: (K2tog, K1) 4 times [8 sts].
rows 56–58: repeat rows 44–46.
row 59: (K2tog) 4 times [4 sts].
rows 60–62: repeat rows 44–46.
row 63: (K2tog) twice [2 sts].
row 64: purl.
row 65: K2tog [1 st].
Sew in the loose ends. Sew the edges together from toe point to top of slipper. (The seam is under the foot and the back of the heel.)

Sometimes, Elizabeth can be heard walking around her little cottage to the sound of tinkling bells.

Breanna

By magically transforming Elizabeth's wardobe from black to bright red, removing the wart and giving her a sweet button nose and pink mouth, you can create Breanna – with her blonde hair tied back in a bow, she is a younger, prettier version of the traditional witch, and perhaps a little less scary too.

Materials and equipment

As for Elizabeth.

Yarns (approximate amounts):
100g (3½oz) cream/flesh coloured for basic body
250g (8¾oz) red for outer clothes and undergarment decorations
50g (1¾oz) white for undergarments
60g (2oz) mixed beige or light brown for hair
small amounts of black, green and pink for face

FACE

Copy Breanna's features from the photograph, or design a new face following the guidelines on page 19. Breanna does not have a crooked nose or a wart!

HAIR

Using 3.00mm (US 3) needles, follow the pattern for the basic hair piece on pages 20–21, but knit rows 5, 11 and 15 instead of loop stitching. Make the loops by wrapping the yarn twice around four fingers initially, and from row 25 onwards wrap the yarn twice around three fingers (see the bottom picture on page 20). This takes some of the weight from the hair piece and, when the loops are cut, the hair will have a 'layered' look.

RIBBON

Cast on 3 sts.
GS for 45cm (17¾in).
Finish off.
Use the ribbon to bunch up Breanna's hair at the back.

LONG-SLEEVED BLOUSE

Breanna has the same blouse as Elizabeth and there is no change in the pattern. Add a tassel to the front point of the collar.

TASSEL

1. Wrap the red yarn around three fingers, 14 times. Take the yarn off your fingers and secure the loops by wrapping a 40cm (15¾in) length of yarn around one end of them. Cut through the loops at the opposite end. Pinch the loops together at the tied end to make a small ball.
2. With one end of the waste yarn, wrap the loops a few more times to secure and sew them into the ball end. With the other end of the waste yarn sew through the ball centre.
3. Add a glass bead that has a hole large enough to pass the yarn through and sew the tassel and bead to the front collar point.

TOP SKIRT

The only difference in the pattern is from row 5 to row 14. These rows are worked in stocking stitch commencing with a knit row, making a flat hem.
Make tassels (without beads) to decorate the hem of Breanna's skirt.

UNDERTOP AND PANTS

Breanna's undertop and pants are the same as Elizabeth's, though knitted in white yarn and decorated with red hearts using duplicate stitch (see page 13).
On her pants, Breanna has heart-shaped pockets, positioned as indicated in the photograph, with a ribbon finish at the top of each heart.

HEART POCKETS

Make two pockets.

Using 3.00mm (US 3) needles, cast on 1 st.
row 1: inc in st [2 sts].
row 2: purl.
row 3: inc in first st, K1 [3 sts].
row 4: purl.
row 5: inc in first 2 sts, K1 [5 sts].
row 6: purl.
row 7: inc in first st, knit to last 2 sts, inc in next st, K1 [7 sts].
row 8: purl.
row 9: repeat row 7.
row 10: purl.
row 11: repeat row 7.
row 12: purl.
row 13: repeat row 7 [13 sts].
row 14: purl.
row 15: K6, turn, P6.
row 16: K5, turn, P5.
row 17: K4, turn, P4.
row 18: K3, turn, P3.
row 19: K2, turn, P2.
row 20: K1, turn, P1.
row 21: cast off 6 sts, knit remaining sts to end [7 sts].
row 22: P6, turn, K6.
row 23: P5, turn, K5.
row 24: P4, turn, K4.
row 25: P3, turn, K3.
row 26: P2, turn, K2.
row 27: P1, turn, K1.
row 28: cast off purlwise.

Finishing off

1. Use the cast-off waste yarn to neaten the centre stitches of the heart.
2. Make four twisted cords of length 15cm (6in), two for each heart (see page 12). Anchor a cord either side of the heart and then thread it through the holes and tie in a bow in the centre.
3. Sew the hearts to the pants, using the photograph for guidance.

SHOES

Breanna prefers Princess Neridah's dainty footwear to Elizabeth's rather old-fashioned walking shoes. Use red yarn and follow the pattern on page 103, though without the embroidery. You may like to make Breanna a pair of red and white comfy slippers too, just for fun!

Mistress Kate

Mistress Kate's more subdued wardrobe of greens, purples and blues transforms her into a kindly country schoolmistress, perhaps, or a fairy godmother. She can be made in any colours you wish, using oddments of yarn.

Copy Kate's features from the photograph, or design a new face using the ideas on page 19. Her hair is the same as Elizabeth's, though I have used grey yarn and 'fluffed it up' to give it a soft, curly appearance. Kate does not have any plaits, but you may put some in if you wish.

Kate's clothes are the same as Elizabeth's, except that the top skirt and the blouse are reversed, so that the inside of the work becomes the outside. This gives her garments a different, pleated effect and the hems are sewn up on the outside.

Kate is a kind, friendly, happy character, and this is reflected in her choice of colourful clothes! Have fun choosing different colours from any oddments of yarn you can find.

Daisy Livingstone Fairy

Daisy Livingstone is a fairy who I originally called simply Daisy, because of the many petals in her dress and jacket. However, having used the lovely pastel shades of lilac, yellow, blue, white and pink, she looked not simply like a daisy but more like a beautiful Livingstone daisy, so I changed her name to Livvy. Change the colours and you may be inspired to give her another daisy name. You could even knit a whole family of flowers!

Livvy's wardrobe consists of a dress, jacket, pants and shoes, all made in five lovely pastel shades. The dress and jacket are fashioned from petal shapes, which form a pretty skirt at the front and cascade down her back. The petal shapes are created by knitting the garments 'sideways', and using partial knitting. Livvy's jacket is finished off with rolled arm and neck edges, and a single button and button loop at the front. When Livvy gives a twirl, which she often does, her petal skirt swings out and shows her pretty petal pants underneath.

All fairies have wings, and Livvy is no exception. They are attached to her jacket at the back and to her arm bracelets. Though they are magnificent wings, her flying can sometimes be a little wobbly, so she has tiny, extra wings around her shoes that she uses to steady herself.

If you wish to add to Livvy's wardrobe, reknit the dress panels and top rib band. You now have a lovely long skirt to match the rest of Livvy's wardrobe.

Begin by knitting the basic body for your doll (see pages 14–18).

Materials and equipment

Needles: one pair each of: 3.00mm (US 3) and 2.25mm (US 1)
Crochet hook: 3.00mm (US 0)
Stitch holders
Needle with eye large enough for yarn, e.g. tapestry needle
Bead-headed pins
Filling: the best quality polyester filling that you can buy
Yarns (approximate amounts):
100g (3½oz) cream/flesh coloured for basic body
50g (1¾oz) brown shades for hair
150g (5¼oz) in total in pink, white, lilac, yellow and blue for clothes and details
small amounts of white, black and pink for face

BASIC PETAL PATTERN

Livvy's dress is made up of twelve petal-shaped panels and her jacket is made up of ten petal-shaped panels. Each panel is made using the basic petal pattern below. Three different sizes of petal are used, known as 5-, 7- and 9-step petals. The basic petal pattern is written for a 5-step petal; to make a 7- or 9- step petal, repeat rows 3, 4, 5 and 6 on the increase and rows 14, 15, 16 and 17 on the decrease. For a 7-step petal repeat them once and for a 9-step petal repeat twice.

Cast on 30 sts for dress and jacket.
row 1: (WS row) purl.
row 2: cast on 2 sts, knit to end.

row 3: knit.
row 4: cast on 2 sts, P12, ytb, sl1, turn.
row 5: ytb, sl1, knit to end.
row 6: cast on 2 sts, K12, sl1, turn, ytb, sl1.
Repeat rows 3–6 once for a 7-step petal and twice for a 9-step petal.

row 7: knit.
row 8: cast on 2 sts, P12, ytb, sl1, turn.
row 9: ytb, sl1, knit to end.
row 10: cast on 2 sts, K20, sl1, turn.
row 11: ytb, sl1, yfwd, purl to end.
row 12: cast off 2 sts purlwise, (with 1 st already on needle) P9, ytb, sl1, turn.
row 13: ytb, sl1, knit to end.

row 14: cast off 2 sts purlwise, (with 1 st already on needle) P9, ytb, sl1, turn.
row 15: ytb, sl1, yfwd, purl to end.
row 16: cast off 2 sts purlwise, (with 1 st already on needle) P9, ytb, sl1, turn.
row 17: ytb, sl1, knit to end.
Repeat rows 14–17 once for a 7-step petal and twice for a 9-step petal.

row 18: cast off 2 sts purlwise, purl to end.
row 19: purl.
row 20: cast off 2 sts purlwise, purl to end.

The inside of the dress, showing how the petal panels are knitted.

FACE

Copy the face shown below, or use your own creativity and make a face of your choosing. Follow the guidelines on page 19. With her antennae-like eyebrows, Livvy resembles a butterfly! Use a single strand of black yarn, and place them just over the eyes. Knot one end, sew the other end into the forehead and fasten off at the back of the head. Make a twisted cord for thicker eyebrows (see page 12).

HAIR

Follow the pattern for the basic hair piece (see pages 20–21), but make the loops by winding the yarn around all four fingers loosely or around two fingers twice. Livvy has curly hair, so do not cut through the loops.

FRINGE

Make the fringe with two-finger loop stitch (see page 21). If desired, trim a little off the front of the hair piece to match the fringe so that the seam is covered as much as possible.

RIBBONS

Using a 3.00mm (US 0) crochet hook, make a number of chains, approximately 40cm (15¾in) long, out of the colours used in the dress and jacket. Knot each end. Gather Livvy's hair up into small bundles and tie the ribbons around them in bows.

DRESS

Livvy's dress consists of four central 5-step petals at the front, then two 7-step petals on each side, and four 9-step petals at the back. The dress is therefore longer at the back than the front.

Using 3.00mm (US 3) needles and following the basic petal pattern on page 46, knit the twelve petal panels in the following order (remember you are knitting the dress sideways):

two 9-step petals; two 7-step petals; four 5-step petals; two 7-step petals; two 9-step petal.

Use a different colour for each petal. Each panel starts and finishes at the top of the bodice, therefore the loose ends need to be woven in here.

When you have completed the twelve panels, make the bodice band.

Tip

Changing colours for each petal leaves many loose ends. You might prefer to sew or weave in the loose ends as you work, rather than have them all to do at the end. This also keeps your work tidier.

BODICE BAND

Use 2.25mm (US 1) needles and white yarn.
With RS facing, pick up 56 sts around the top edge of the bodice.
Rib (K1, P1) for 6 rows.
Cast off ribwise.
Sew up the back seam of the dress and bodice band.

SHOULDER STRAPS

Make two straps.
Using 3.00mm (US 3) needles and white yarn, cast on 4 sts.
GS for 32 rows.
Cast off.
Attach the straps to the inside of the bodice, along the band seam.

The completed dress is shown on the following page.

This gorgeous dress is snug fitting, and is allowed to be this way because the doll is so soft and flexible. If your doll has big hair, dress her feet-first. She will look simply stunning while she is waiting for you to knit her jacket.

The completed dress.

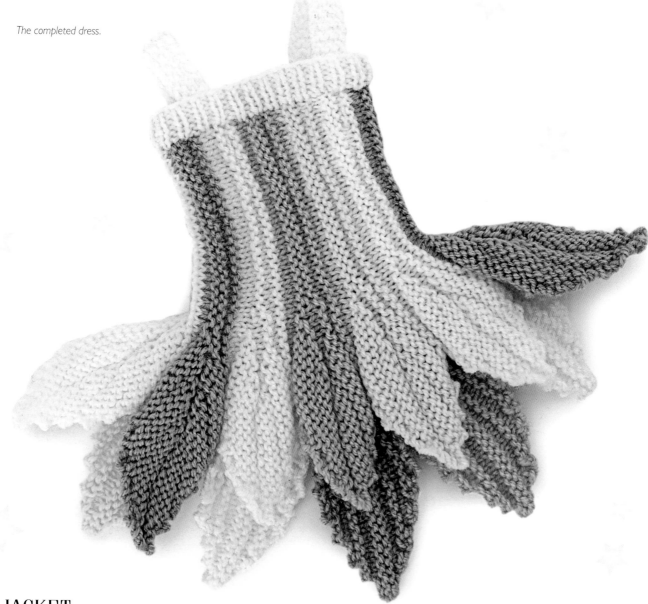

JACKET

Like her dress, Livvy's jacket hangs longer at the back than the front. Once again, it is knitted sideways and uses partial knitting to create the petal shapes.

The jacket consists of four 5-step petals at the front, two 7-step petals on each side of these, and two 9-step petals at the back. It is knitted using 3.00mm (US 3) needles in pink, white, lilac, yellow and blue. Loose ends are created at the neck edge when joining in and breaking off the different coloured yarns. Sewing in the loose ends as you go keeps your work tidy and easier to handle.

Cast on 30 sts in pink.
Commencing with row 1 of the basic petal pattern, complete two 5-step petals, changing to white for the second petal.

SHAPE LEFT-HAND ARMHOLE

Continue with the same colour yarn and cast off 20 sts. Break yarn.

Join in the lilac yarn and purl to end (becomes row 1 of next petal).
next row: cast on 2 sts, knit 12 sts and cast on 20 sts (becomes row 2 of basic petal pattern).
Continue from row 3 of basic petal pattern and complete two 7-step petals, changing to yellow on the second panel.

BACK NECKLINE

Cast off 5 sts with the yellow yarn. Break yarn.
Join in the blue yarn and purl to end (becomes row 1 of next petal).
Complete two 9-step petals, changing to pink on the second panel. Break yarn.
With white yarn, cast on 5 sts (neckline complete).
Complete two 7-step petals, changing to lilac on the second panel.

The completed wings, attached to Livvy's jacket and arm bracelets.

Flamenka

Flamenka is a fiery Mediterranean version of Livvy. She is knitted in shades of yellow, orange and white and her wings and clothes are embellished with sparkling gold accents. The patterns are the same as those used for Livvy's clothes – simply change the colours and decorate with sparkly gold fabric glue.

Copy the face shown in the photographs on this page, or create a face of your own (see page 19). For her hair, use black yarn and follow the basic pattern on pages 20–21. Her hair is created by wrapping the yarn four times around four fingers to form long loops. It is then tied up in bunches, high up on her head, using single strands of orange yarn and gold thread for ribbons. Because the hair will be quite heavy, make sure that the neck is not too narrow – a wider neck will hold the hair better.

This lovely fiery character is full of life and sparkle, reminiscent of a fire fairy, or a Spanish flamenco dancer.

Samuel Crowe Pirate

Samuel Crowe loves being a swashbuckling pirate, and especially the freedom of sailing the oceans in his ship, Deep Silver. No-one really knows whether he has ever been to the Caribbean, but he often talks about St Lucia as if he had been there many times.

Samuel is a flamboyant dresser, and likes to wear silks and fine clothes, though he does not always look after them. His silk shirt protects his skin from the rather harsher fabric of his jacket, and he loves the frills on the cuffs. His hair, which is weaved into dreadlocks, is decorated with beads that he has acquired on his many voyages.

Begin by knitting the basic body for your doll (see pages 14–18).

Materials and equipment

Needles: one pair each of: 3.00mm (US 3) and 2.25mm (US 1)

Crochet hook: 3.00mm (US 0)

Stitch holders and optional 2.25mm (US 1) double-pointed needles

Needle with eye large enough for yarn, e.g. tapestry needle

Bead-headed pins

Filling: the best quality polyester filling that you can buy

White chenille sticks

Various beads with large holes

Yarns (approximate amounts):
100g (3½oz) cream/flesh coloured for basic body
100g (3½oz) medium blue for jacket
80g (2¾oz) black for hair
50g (1¾oz) medium brown for breeches
30g (1oz) white for shirt
30g (1oz) dark blue for tricorn hat
50g (1¾oz) dark brown for boots
small amounts of medium and dark brown, burgundy, pink and grey for sword, belts and scarves; black, white and red for face; gold for rings

FACE

Copy Samuel's face from the photograph below, or create one of your own following the guidelines on page 19. His moustache is made up of a number of short, angled stitches, and his small beard is four short, uneven vertical stitches placed just below his mouth. The long beard is made separately using double loop stitch and fashioned once it is attached to Samuel's chin.

LONG BEARD

Using 2.25mm (US 1) needles and black yarn, cast on 19 sts. Making the width of each loop a generous four fingers, and pull each loop stitch to secure it firmly.
row 1: LS for the first st and every alt st to end.
Cast off.
Turn in and sew under the cast-on edge to hide it, and sew this edge to the chin. Cut the loops and tease out the strands. Separate the beard into two bunches. Make these into two small dreadlocks (see below, right).

HAIR

1. Using 3.00mm (US 3) needles and black yarn, make the basic hair piece with four-finger loops (see page 21). Fit the hair to Samuel's head. Pin in place and, when you are happy with the look, sew the hair securely to the head.

2. Cut through the loops unevenly to create different lengths of hair. This will give Samuel a more untidy hair style, as befits someone who spends a lot of time at sea.
3. Take five or six extra strands of yarn, approximately 10cm (4in) in length, and separate the ply to make thinner strands. Make a knot about 2cm (¾in) from one end of each strand and thread on some beads. Sew the unknotted end into the hair piece. Place the beaded strands around the head so that they are clearly visible.
4. Make dreadlocks with extra pieces of yarn (see below) and sew these into the hair on each side of the head, at different levels.
5. If you wish, make some plaits, add beads and once again sew them into the hair.

DREADLOCKS

Hold a bunch of yarn and bind it tightly with a longer piece of yarn of the same colour. Thread this length of yarn into a needle and push it up through the dreadlock. Secure the yarn to stop it unwinding.

JACKET

Samuel's jacket is knitted in garter stitch, which gives a good, firm fabric. The back is split to the waist and the front of the jacket has embroidered buttons, buttonholes and flap pockets. The full sleeves end just above Samuel's wrists so that he can show off the lace edging on the sleeves of his flamboyant shirt underneath.

LEFT FRONT

Using 3.00mm (US 3) needles and medium blue yarn, cast on 32 sts.
rows 1–6: GS.
row 7: K10, K2tog, K8, K2tog tbl, K10 [30 sts].
rows 8–13: GS.
row 14: K9, K2tog, K8, K2tog tbl, K9 [28 sts].
rows 15–20: GS.
row 21: K8, K2tog, K8, K2tog tbl, K8 [26 sts].
rows 22–27: GS.
row 28: K7, K2tog, K8, K2tog tbl, K7 [24 sts].
rows 29–34: GS.
row 35: K7, K2tog, K6, K2tog tbl, K7 [22 sts].
rows 36–41: GS.
row 42: K6, K2tog, K6, K2tog tbl, K6 [20 sts].
rows 43–48: GS.
row 49: K5, K2tog, K6, K2tog tbl, K5 [18 sts].
rows 50–55: GS.
row 56: K5, K2tog, K4, K2tog tbl, K5 [16 sts].
rows 57–72: GS.
Mark each end of row 72 with waste yarn to indicate the waistline.
rows 73–87: GS.

Armhole shaping

row 88: cast off 3 sts, knit to end [13 sts].
rows 89–102: GS.

Shaping the neckline

row 103: cast off 3 sts, knit to end [10 sts].
row 104: knit.
row 105: K2tog, knit to end [9 sts].
row 106: knit.
row 107: K2tog, knit to end [8 sts].
rows 108–109: GS.
Cast off.

RIGHT FRONT

Knit as for left front, omitting row 72.

POCKET FLAPS

Make two.

Using 2.25mm (US 1) needles, cast on 6 sts.
row 1: knit.
row 2: cast off 1 st, knit to end [5 sts].
row 3: knit.
row 4: cast off 1 st, knit to end.
row 5: knit.
row 6: cast on 1 st, knit to end.
row 7: knit.
row 8: cast on 1 st, knit to end.
row 9: knit.
row 10: cast off 1 st, knit to end.
row 11: knit.
row 12: cast off 1 st, knit to end.
row 13: knit.
row 14: cast on 1 st, knit to end.
row 15: knit.
row 16: cast on 1 st [6 sts].
Cast off.

Jacket front

Jacket back

BUTTONS AND BUTTONHOLES

Embroider the buttons and buttonholes before making up the jacket.

1. On each side of the jacket front, mark two rows down from the neck and every sixth row after that down the jacket edge. Use these marks to position the buttons on one side of the jacket and buttonholes on the other.
2. Use a simple two-stranded satin stitch for the buttonholes. Use French knots, made by winding the yarn six times around the needle, for the buttons.
3. Weave in the loose ends to secure them.

BACK

The skirt of the jacket back is split to give Samuel plenty of freedom to move and attend to his sword. Both sides are the same and are joined at row 72.

Cast on 32 sts.
Repeat rows 1–71 of jacket left front [16 sts].
Break yarn and put the sts on to a stitch holder.

Cast on 32 sts.
Repeat rows 1–72 of jacket left front [16 sts].
Replace the held sts on to the LH needle.
Continue row 72 by knitting the replaced LH needle sts [32 sts].
Mark each end of this row to indicate the waistline.
rows 73–87: GS.

Armhole shaping

row 88: cast off 3 sts, knit to end.
row 89: repeat row 88 [26 sts].
rows 90–102: GS.

Shaping the neckline

row 103: K10, cast off 6 sts, knit to end.
Continue on the last 10 sts.
row 104: knit.
row 105: K2tog, knit to end.
row 106: knit.
row 107: K2tog, knit to end [8 sts].
row 108: knit.
Cast off.
Break yarn. Rejoin yarn at neck edge to remaining 10 sts on LH needle.
row 104: knit.
row 105: K8, K2tog [9 sts].
row 106: knit.
row 107: K7, K2tog [8 sts].
row 108: knit.
Cast off.
To finish off the back opening, just above the join make a long, double-yarn satin stitch and put two small French knots at either end for buttons.

MAKING UP

With WS facing, oversew the jacket shoulder seams. This allows the seams to be flattened nicely.

NECKLINE EDGE

1. Using 2.25mm (US 1) needles and with RS facing, pick up 10 sts along the right front edge of the neckline, 18 sts along the back neck edge and 10 sts along the left front edge [38 sts].
2. Cast off.
3. Weave in the loose ends and secure.

SLEEVES

Using 3.00mm (US 3) needles, cast on 35 sts.
rows 1–40: GS.
row 41: purl (turning row for the cuff).
rows 42–43: GS.
row 44: K1, inc in next st, knit to last 2 sts, inc in next st, K1 [37 sts].
row 45: knit.
rows 46–51: repeat rows 44 and 45, 3 times [43 sts].
rows 52–59: GS for 8 rows.
Cast off.
Sew in the loose ends. Embroider the sleeve cuffs with buttonholes and buttons.

The completed sleeve, before making up, shown in a lighter colour so that the embroidery can be seen clearly.

MAKING UP

Attach the pocket flaps to the right and left fronts of the jacket, as indicated in the photographs on the previous page. Oversew the jacket side seams up to the armhole. Turn the jacket inside-out and place the sleeves in the armholes from inside the jacket. Pin the sleeves to the jacket then stitch them in place, matching the jacket and sleeve seams.

BREECHES

The legs of Samuel's breeches are knitted separately and then joined for the body section. The breeches have a front flap which is fastened with a button and loop. There is a knitted strip up the side of each leg and the front flap is edged with two knitted stitches on each side.

RIGHT LEG

Using medium brown yarn and 3.00mm (US 3) needles, cast on 30 sts.
rows 1–3: GS.
row 4: knit.
row 5: P14, K2, P14.
rows 6–41: repeat rows 4 and 5, 18 times.
Break yarn. Put the sts on to a stitch holder or spare needle.

LEFT LEG

Using 3.00mm (US 3) needles, cast on 30 sts.
Repeat rows 1–41 of right leg.
row 42: knit.
Replace the sts held on the stitch holder on to the LH needle and continue knitting across these sts (this completes row 42 and joins both legs together) [60 sts].

The button and loop fastening on the left-hand side of Samuel's breeches. The knitted strips up the side of the leg and flap can also be seen.

row 43: P14, K2, P28, K2, P14.
row 44: knit.
rows 45–48: repeat rows 43 and 44, twice.
row 49: repeat row 43.

SHAPE THE FRONT FLAP

row 50: K40, turn.
row 51: cast on 2 sts, K2, P20, turn.
row 52: cast on 2 sts, K24.
These 24 sts are used for the front flap; put the other sts on to a stitch holder.
row 53: knit [24 sts].
row 54: K2, P20, K2.
rows 55–66: repeat rows 53 and 54, 6 times.
row 67: repeat row 53.

Change to 2.25mm (US 1) needles.
row 68: K2, (K2tog) to last 2 sts, K2 [14 sts].
row 69: K2, (K1, P1) to last 2 sts, K2.
rows 70–71: repeat row 69, twice.
Cast off in pattern.

Replace sts for RHS of breeches held on stitch holder on to needle.
Using 3.00mm (US 3) needles, rejoin yarn [20 sts].
row 50: cast on 2 sts, knit to end [22 sts].
row 51: P14, K2, P4, K2.
row 52: knit.
rows 53–66: repeat rows 51 and 52, 7 times.
row 67: repeat row 52.

Change to 2.25mm (US 1) needles.
row 68: K2, (K2tog) to last 2 sts, K2 [13 sts].
row 69: K1, (K1, P1) to last 2 sts, K2.

rows 70–71: K2, (K1, P1) to last st, K1.
Cast off in pattern.
Replace sts for LHS of breeches held on stitch holder on to the needle.
Using 3.00mm (US 3) needles, rejoin yarn [20 sts].
row 51: cast on 2 sts, P4, K2, P14 [22 sts].
row 52: knit.
row 53: K2, P4, K2, P14.
rows 54–67: repeat rows 52 and 53, 7 times.

Change to 2.25mm (US 1) needles.
row 68: K2, (K2tog) to last 2 sts, K2 [13 sts].

Samuel's breeches are just long enough to fit inside his boots.

row 69: K1, (K1, P1) to end.
row 70: (K1, P1) to last st, K1.
row 71: repeat row 69.
Cast off in pattern.

MAKING UP

Sew together the leg edge seams and back seam of the body. Lay the body flap over the top part of the breeches so that the sides of the flap overlap the two stitches on either front edge of the breeches. Sew the bottom of the flap to the edges for about 1cm (½in).

BUTTON AND LOOP FASTENING

Make two bobble buttons (see below) and sew them to the front edges of the breeches at the waist. Make a loop on each side of the flap to match. Sew around each loop with buttonhole stitch.

Button

Using 2.25mm (US 1) needles, cast on 3 sts.
row 1: inc in each st [6 sts].
rows 2–5: knit.
row 6: (K2tog) to end [3 sts].
Cast off.
Sew around the edge of the button and gather tightly to finish off.

SHIRT

Samuel's shirt has long, full sleeves, and the pointed collar is big and loose. It gives Samuel plenty of room to move when brandishing his sword!

FRONT

Using white yarn and 3.00mm (US 3) needles, cast on 26 sts.
rows 1–4: GS.
rows 5–16: SS, commencing with a knit row.
row 17: P12, K2, P12.
row 18: knit.
row 19: P10, K6, P10.

Armhole shaping

row 20: cast off 3 sts, (with 1 st on needle) K9, turn [10 sts].
Continue on these 10 sts.
row 21: K3, purl to end.
row 22: knit.
rows 23–30: repeat rows 21 and 22, 4 times.

Shaping the neckline

row 31: cast off 3 sts, purl to end [7 sts].
row 32: K5, K2tog [6 sts].
row 33: purl.
row 34: knit.
row 35: purl.
Cast off.

The completed shirt.

With RS facing, rejoin yarn to the right front.
row 20: knit to end.

Armhole shaping

row 21: cast off 3 sts, (with 1 st on needle) P6, K3 [10 sts).
row 22: knit.
row 23: P7, K3.
rows 24–31: repeat rows 22 and 23, 4 times.

Shaping the neckline

row 32: cast off 3 sts, knit to end [7 sts].
row 33: P5, P2tog [6 sts].
row 34: knit.
row 35: purl.
row 36: knit.
Cast off purlwise.
Sew in the loose ends.

BACK

The back is similar to the shirt front, but without the neck opening.

Using 3.00mm (US 3) needles, cast on 26 sts.
rows 1–4: GS.
rows 5–19: SS, commencing with a knit row.

Armhole shaping

row 20: cast off 3 sts purlwise, purl to end [23 sts].
row 21: cast off 3 sts, knit to end [20 sts].
rows 22–32: SS, commencing with a purl row.

Shaping the neckline

row 33: K7, cast off 6 sts, (with 1 st on needle) K6.
Using the first 7 sts on the needle:
row 34: P5, P2tog [6 sts].
row 35: knit.

row 36: purl.
Cast off.
With WS facing, rejoin yarn at the neck edge of right back.
row 34: P2tog, purl to end of row [6 sts].
row 35: knit.
row 36: purl.
Cast off.
Sew in the loose ends. Sew up the shoulder seams and side seams.

SLEEVES

Make two.

Using 3.00mm (US 3) needles, cast on 35 sts.
Commencing at the wrist edge:
row 1: (K1, K2tog, K1, yfwd, K1) to end.
row 2: knit.
row 3: repeat row 1.
row 4: purl.
row 5: knit.
row 6: purl.
row 7: K1, (K2tog) to end [18 sts].
row 8: purl.
row 9: inc 1 st in each st [36 sts].
rows 10–45: SS, commencing with a purl row. Decrease 1 st at each end of rows 15, 21, 27 and 33 [28 sts].
Cast off.

MAKING UP

1. Sew the sleeve edges together. For each sleeve, place the sleeve in the armhole RS facing. Match the sleeve seam with the side seam of the shirt. Pin the sleeve in place and sew using back stitch.
2. Make a 30cm (11¾in) cord for each sleeve (see page 12) and weave it into the wristline, commencing and finishing at the seam. Pull together and tie into a bow.

COLLAR

The first two or three rows will be a little tight. The knitting loosens up as the collar gets wider.

row 1: with RS facing, pick up and knit 8 sts along the right front edge of the neckline, 15 sts along the back neck edge, and 8 sts along the left front neck edge [31 sts].
row 2: K1, inc in next st, (K6, inc in next st) 4 times, K1 [36 sts].
row 3: knit.
row 4: K1, inc in next st, (K7, inc in next st) twice, K8, inc in next st, K7, inc in next st, K1 [41 sts].
row 5: knit.
row 6: K1, inc in next st, K8, inc in next st, (K9, inc in next st) twice, K8, inc in next st, K1 [46 sts].
row 7: knit.
row 8: K1, (inc in next st, K10) 3 times, K9, inc in next st, K1 [51 sts].
row 9: knit.
row 10: K1, inc in next st, (K11, inc in next st) 4 times, K1 [56 sts].
row 11: knit.
Cast off loosely (or use a larger needle). Sew in the loose ends.

> ## Tip
>
> To match the points of the collar, put the point of a needle into each one and pull gently to even out the stitches.

BOOTS

Samuel's handsome boots have long legs and he wears them turned down from the knee. The instep is shaped at the centre of the work and the edges of the work become the centre back of the boot.

Make two boots.

SOLE

Using 2.25mm (US 1) needles and dark brown yarn, cast on 6 sts.
row 1: inc in first st, K3, inc in next st, K1 [8 sts].
row 2: knit.
row 3: inc in first st, K5, inc in next st, K1 [10 sts].
rows 4–20: GS.
row 21: K4, K2tog, K4 [9 sts].
rows 22–24: GS.
row 25: K3, K2tog, K4 [8 sts].
row 26: knit.
row 27: K3, K2tog, K3 [7 sts].
rows 28–29: GS.
row 30: K3, K2tog, K2 [6 sts].
rows 31–32: GS.
Cast off.
Sew in the loose ends.

LEG

Using 2.25mm (US 1) needles, cast on 48 sts.
row 1: K21, K2tog tbl, K2, K2tog, K21 [46 sts].
row 2: P20, P2tog, P2, P2tog, P20 [44 sts].
row 3: K19, K2tog, K2, K2tog, K19 [42 sts].
row 4: P18, P2tog, P2, P2tog, P18 [40 sts].
row 5: K17, K2tog tbl, K2, K2tog, K17 [38 sts].
row 6: P16, P2tog, P2, P2tog, P16 [36 sts].
row 7: K15, K2tog tbl, K2, K2tog, K15 [34 sts].
row 8: P14, P2tog, P2, P2tog, P14 [32 sts].
row 9: K13, K2tog tbl, K2, K2tog, K13 [30 sts].
row 10: purl.
rows 11–46: SS, commencing with a knit row.
row 47: K2, inc in next st, (K4, inc in next st) 5 times, K2 [36 sts].
rows 48–51: GS.
row 52: K3, inc in next st, (K4, inc in next st) 6 times, K2 [43 sts].
rows 53–56: GS.
row 57: K1, inc in next st, (K4, inc in next st) 8 times, K1 [52 sts].
rows 58–61: GS.
row 62: K3, inc in next st, (K4, inc in next st) 9 times, K3 [62 sts].
rows 63–70: GS.
row 71: K3, inc in next st, (K4, inc in next st) 11 times, K3 [74 sts].
rows 72–77: GS.
Cast off loosely or use a larger needle.

MAKING UP

Sew the back seam of the boot, including the cuff, keeping in mind that the cuff turns over and becomes the outside of the boot leg. Pin the sole to the leg, matching the centre back seam and centre back of heel. Oversew the sole to the boot.

TRICORN HAT

Start knitting the hat at the brim.

Using 3.00mm (US 3) needles and dark blue yarn, cast on 160 sts.
row 1: knit.
row 2: (K8, K2tog) to end [144 sts].
row 3: knit.
row 4: (K8, K2tog) to last 4 sts, K4 [130 sts].
row 5: knit.
row 6: (K8, K2tog) to end [117 sts].
row 7: knit.
row 8: (K8, K2tog) to last 7 sts, K7 [106 sts].
row 9: knit.
row 10: (K8, K2tog) to last 6 sts, K6 [96 sts].
row 11: knit.
row 12: (K8, K2tog) to last 6 sts, K6 [87 sts].
row 13: knit.
row 14: (K8, K2tog) to last 7 sts, K7 [79 sts].
row 15: knit.
row 16: (K8, K2tog) to last 9 sts, K9 [72 sts].
rows 17–27: SS, commencing with a knit row.
row 28: purl.
row 29: (K8, K2tog) to last 2 sts, K2 [65 sts].
row 30: purl.
row 31: (K8, K2tog) to last 5 sts, K5 [59 sts].
row 32: purl.
row 33: (K8, K2tog) to last 9 sts, K9 [54 sts].
row 34: purl.
row 35: (K8, K2tog) to last 4 sts, K4 [49 sts].
row 36: purl.
row 37: (K8, K2tog) to last 9 sts, K9 [45 sts].
row 38: purl.
row 39: (K8, K2tog) to last 3 sts, K3 [38 sts].
row 40: purl.
row 41: (K8, K2tog) to last 2 sts, K2 [29 sts].
row 42: purl.
row 43: (K8, K2tog) to last 2 sts, K2 [20 sts].
row 44: purl.
row 45: (K8, K2tog) to last 2 sts, K2 [14 sts].
row 46: (P2tog) to end [7 sts].

Break yarn, leaving a 30cm (11¾in) tail. Thread the yarn through the remaining 7 sts and finish off tightly. Continue to sew the edges of the hat together down to the beginning of the brim. Using the cast-on waste yarn, sew the brim. As it is turned up to form the three corners of the hat, make the underside the RS.

BRIM REINFORCEMENT

Using 3.00mm (US 3) needles and dark blue yarn, cast on 140 sts.
Cast off.

MAKING UP

1. Join the edges of the reinforcement and pin it to the outside edge of the brim to stiffen it. Sew it in place.
2. Fold the brim up equally in three places to form the tricorn hat. Fix the centre of each folded section to the hat crown with a large cross stitch. This will keep the brim in place.
3. Pinch the corners of the brim and secure with a couple of hidden stitches.

HEAD SCARF

The head scarf is knitted using partial knitting.
Using 3.00mm (US 3) needles and burgundy yarn, cast on 140 sts.
rows 1–3: GS.
row 4: K95, yfwd, sl1, turn, yfwd, sl1, P50, ytb, sl1, turn, ytb, sl1, K45, yfwd, sl1, turn, yfwd, sl1, P40, ytb, sl1, turn, ytb, sl1, K90.
rows 5–7: GS.
(For a narrower scarf, cast off here.)
row 8: repeat row 4.
rows 9–11: GS.
Cast off loosely.
Sew in the loose ends.

BELT

Using 2.25mm (US 1) needles and dark brown yarn, cast on 5 sts. GS for 25cm (9¾in).
next row: K2tog, K1, K2tog tbl [3 sts].
next row: K2tog, K1, pass first st over second st.
Finish off.
Sew in the loose ends.

BUCKLE

Trim a chenille stick to length 14cm (5½in), and shape it as shown to form the inside of the buckle. The central bar (formed from the two ends of the chenille stick) should be 2cm (¾in) long. Tie yarn around the two parts of the central bar to hold them together whilst attaching the buckle cover.

Buckle cover

Using medium brown yarn, cast on 25 sts.
row 1: (RS row) knit.
row 2: purl.
rows 3–6: knit.
row 7: purl.
Cast off.

MAKING UP

1. Keeping the RS of the work on the outside, sew the short edges of the buckle cover together. This makes the work into a circle, which will fit neatly over the buckle shape. Sew the cast-on and cast-off edges together at the centre of the buckle.
2. Stitch around the central bar, placing a few long, vertical stitches across the bar and catching them on either side of the buckle to keep the buckle in shape and the central bar firm. Sew buttonhole stitches around the central bar and the long stitches.
3. Sew the unshaped (cast-on) end of the belt to the back of the central bar.

SWORD BELT AND SWORD

SWORD BELT

Using 3.00mm (US 3) needles and dark brown yarn, cast on 6 sts. GS for 40cm (15¾in).
next row: K2tog, K2, K2tog tbl [4 sts].
next row: K2tog, K2tog tbl [2 sts].
next row: K2tog.
Finish off.
Weave in the loose ends.

Samuel is always ready for some swashbuckling action!

Sword belt buckle

Trace off the buckle shape (shown below, actual size). Make a buckle out of card or thin plastic.

Using 2.25mm (US 1) needles and medium brown yarn, cast on 34 sts.
row 1: knit.
row 2: purl.
row 3: K1, (yrn, K2tog) to last st, yrn, K1 [35 sts].
row 4: purl.
row 5: knit.
row 6: purl.
Cast off.

Sword sleeve

Using 2.25mm (US 1) needles and medium brown yarn, cast on 12 sts.
row 1: knit.
row 2: K3, P6, K3.
rows 3–18: repeat rows 1 and 2, 8 times.
Cast off.

Making up

1. Sew the short edges of the buckle cover together. This makes the work into a circle which will fit neatly over the cut-out buckle shape.
2. Pinch the cast-on and cast-off edges on the inside of the buckle, and sew.
3. Cover the central bar using buttonhole stitch.
4. Sew the non-pointed end of the sword belt to the central bar.
5. Sew the cast-on and cast-off edges of the sword sleeve together. Sew this seam to the centre of the sword belt, 10cm (4in) from the centre of the buckle. Slot the sword into the sword sleeve when not in use.

SWORD

I have used an I-cord (see page 13) to make the sword because it gives a flat, smooth finish. Give the work a little pull and twist as you knit to even out the stitches and to make the work easier to measure.

Using double-pointed 2.25mm (US 1) needles and grey yarn, cast on 6 sts.
Make an I-cord 4cm (1½in) in length, following the instructions on page 13 (this will be the hilt of the sword).
next row: K2, sl1, K1, psso, K2 [5 sts].

To shape the point of the sword:
next row: K1, K2tog, K2 [4 sts].
next row: K1, K2tog, K1 [3 sts].
next row: K2tog, K1 [2 sts].
next row: K2tog.
Finish off, and sew in the loose ends.

Hand guard

Using 2.25mm (US 1) needles and medium brown yarn, cast on 3 sts.
row 1: knit.
row 2: inc in first 2 sts [5 sts].
row 3: knit.
row 4: K1, (inc in next st, K1) twice [7 sts].
row 5: K3, K2tog, K2 [6 sts].
row 6: K3, yrn twice, K3.
row 7: knit (knitting only once in fourth st) [7 sts].
row 8: K2, P3, K2.
row 9: knit.
rows 10–25: repeat rows 8 and 9, 8 times.
row 26: K3, K2tog, K2 [6 sts].
row 27: K3, yrn twice, K3.
row 28: knit (knitting only once in fourth st) [7 sts].
row 29: K1, K2tog, K1, K2tog tbl, K1 [5 sts].
row 30: knit.
row 31: K2tog, K1, K2tog tbl [3 sts].
Cast off.
Sew in the loose ends.

Making up

1. Trim a chenille stick to just over 21cm (8¼in) in length and bend over the tip of the wire at each end, making it safer to use and easier to push into the knitted cord. Carefully push the chenille stick through the sword to the pointed end. You may need to twist the stick gently as you push.
2. At the hilt end, leaving a 0.5cm (¼in) gap at the top, create a small hand grip by winding grey yarn tightly around the sword for about 2.5cm (1in).
3. With the right side of the hand guard on the outside, push the hand grip through the holes made at each end of the hand guard. Spread out the hand guard so that it covers each end of the hand grip.

BELT SCARF

Samuel's pink scarf is worn over his belt. He likes the way it swishes from side to side as he walks. The scarf was a gift and it is one of the few things that Samuel wears all the time.

Using 2.25mm (US 1) needles, cast on 1 st.
row 1: inc in first st [2 sts].
row 2: knit.
row 3: K1, inc in next st [3 sts].
row 4: knit.
row 5: K2, inc in next st [4 sts].
row 6: knit.
row 7: K3, inc in next st [5 sts].
row 8: knit.
row 9: K4, inc in next st [6 sts].
row 10: knit.
row 11: K4, P1, inc in next st [7 sts].
row 12: knit.
row 13: K4, P1, K1, inc in next st [8 sts].
row 14: knit.

row 15: K4, P1, K2, inc in next st [9 sts].
row 16: knit.
row 17: K4, P1, K2, P1, inc in next st [10 sts].
row 18: knit.
row 19: K4, P1, K2, P1, K2.
row 20: knit.
rows 21–40: repeat rows 19 and 20, 10 times.
row 41: K2, K2tog, P1, K2, P1, K2 [9 sts].
row 42: knit.
row 43: K3, P1, K2, P1, K2.
rows 44–53: repeat rows 42 and 43, 5 times.
row 54: knit.
row 55: K1, K2tog, P1, K2, P1, K2 [8 sts].
row 56: knit.
row 57: K2, P1, K2, P1, K2.
rows 58–71: repeat rows 56 and 57, 7 times.
row 72: knit.
row 73: K2tog, P1, K2, P1, K2 [7 sts].
row 74: K2tog, knit to end [6 sts].
row 75: K1, P1, K2, P1, K1.
row 76: knit.
rows 77–84: repeat rows 75 and 76, 4 times.
rows 85–86: knit.
row 87: K1, P1, K2, P1, K1.
rows 88–101: repeat rows 86 and 87, 7 times.
row 102: knit.
row 103: inc in first st, P1 K2, P1, K1 [7 sts].
row 104: knit.
row 105: K2, P1, K2, P1, K1.
rows 106–109: repeat rows 104 and 105, twice.
row 110: knit.
row 111: inc in first st, K1, P1, K2, P1, K1 [8 sts].
row 112: knit.
row 113: K3, P1, K2, P1, K1.
rows 114–117: repeat rows 112 and 113, twice.
row 118: knit.
row 119: K2tog, K1, P1, K2, P1, K1 [7 sts].
row 120: knit.
row 121: K2tog, P1, K2, P1, K1 [6 sts].
row 122: knit.
row 123: K2tog, K2, P1, K1 [5 sts].
row 124: knit.
row 125: K2tog, K1, P1, K1 [4 sts].
row 126: knit.
row 127: K2tog, P1, K1 [3 sts].
row 128: knit.
row 129: K2tog, K1 [2 sts].
row 130: knit.
row 131: K2tog [1 st].
Finish off.
Sew in the loose ends.

RINGS

Samuel's rings are made using gold yarn and 2.25mm
(US 1) needles.
Cast on 6 sts.
next row: K2, P2, K2.
Cast off.
Sew the sides of the ring together and sew in the loose ends
(this is easier to do if you place the ring over a 4mm/US 6
needle). The rings can be decorated with dimensional paints or
self-adhesive gemstones.

*Samuel completes his outfit with
two gold rings, one on each hand,
which he brought home from one
of his voyages. To place a ring on
his finger, thread the ring on to
a 2.25mm (US 1) needle, then
push the tip of the needle into
Sam's fingertips and transfer the
ring to his finger – the ring is a
good fit!*

Alistair Wizard

No-one knows quite how old Alistair Wizard is, but judging by his long, grey hair and beard, he is very old indeed. His long, purple cloak with its gold embroidery gives him a regal air, and he has a matching pointed hat that is similar in many ways to that of Elizabeth Witch, with whom he is good friends. The back of Alistair's cloak is longer than the front and drapes nicely over his tunic, and it billows out behind him as he hurries across the cold, flag-stoned floors of his castle.

Even though his cloak is very warm, Alistair is happy to wear his long pants and woolly tunic as well to add to his comfort during the cold winter months. His bright yellow, pointed shoes with turn-down cuffs are warm and cosy, but he also has some very fashionable sandals for the sunnier months of the year. On his right hand he wears a mysterious gold ring with a large purple stone and a gold bracelet, both as ancient as the aged wizard himself. They are identical to Daisy Livingstone Fairy's rings and bracelets (see page 52), but using purple for the flower button.

Begin by knitting the basic body for your doll (see pages 14–18).

Materials and equipment

Needles: two pairs of 3.00mm (US 3), one long and one short, and one pair of 2.25mm (US 1)

Crochet hook: 3.00mm (US 0)

Stitch holders and optional 2.25mm (US 1) double-pointed needles

Needle with eye large enough for yarn, e.g. tapestry needle

Bead-headed pins

Filling: the best quality polyester filling that you can buy

Yarns (approximate amounts):
100g (3½oz) cream/flesh coloured for basic body
150g (5¼oz) purple for cloak, hat and shoes
100g (3½oz) in total in lilac mix and yellow for tunic and pants
100g (3½oz) light grey for hair
small amounts of yellow, purple and lilac for embroidery and belt, and black, white, blue and red for face

FACE

Embroider the eyes and a small, red mouth following the photograph below and the instructions on page 19.

HAIR

Alistair's long, wispy hair is made using fewer loop stitches than usual, following the pattern given below. Each loop is made by wrapping the yarn twice around four fingers. Cut the loops unevenly to give Alistair a wild, untidy appearance.

Using 3.00mm (US 3) needles and light grey yarn, cast on 16 sts (this is the nape of the neck).
row 1: LS to end.
row 2: K1, inc in next st, K12, inc in next st, K1 [18 sts].
row 3: knit.
row 4: K1, inc in next st, K14, inc in next st, K1 [20 sts].
row 5: LS to end.
row 6: K1, inc in next st, K16, inc in next st, K1 [22 sts].
row 7: knit.
row 8: K20, sl1, turn, ytb, K14, sl1, turn, ytb, K12, sl1, turn, ytb, sl1, LS10, sl1, turn, ytb, sl1, knit to end.
row 9: LS to end.
row 10: K1, inc in next st, K18, inc in next st, K1 [24 sts].
row 11: LS to end.
row 12: knit.
row 13: LS to end.
row 14: K22, sl1, turn, ytb, K16, sl1, turn, ytb, K14, sl1, turn, ytb, sl1, LS12, sl1, turn, ytb, sl1, knit to end.
row 15: knit.
row 16: knit.
row 17: LS to end.
row 18: knit.
row 19: LS4, K16, LS4.
row 20: K22, sl1, turn, ytb, K16, sl1, turn, ytb, K14, sl1, turn, ytb, sl1, LS12, sl1, turn, ytb, sl1, knit to end.
row 21: LS8, K8, LS8.
row 22: knit.
row 23: LS to end.
row 24: K1, K2tog, K18, K2tog tbl, K1 [22 sts].
row 25: knit.
row 26: K1, K2tog, K16, K2tog tbl, K1 [20 sts].

row 27: LS to end.
row 28: K1, K2tog, K14, K2tog tbl, K1 [18 sts].
row 29: K18, sl1, turn, ytb, K14, sl1, turn, ytb, K12, sl1, turn, ytb, sl1, LS10, sl1, turn, ytb, sl1, knit to end.
row 30: knit.
row 31: LS to end.
row 32: K1, (K2tog) twice, K8, (K2tog tbl) twice, K1 [14 sts].
row 33: LS to end.
row 34: (K2tog) to end [7 sts].
row 35: LS to end.
row 36: LS2, (pass first knitted st over second st, LS1) repeat to end.
Finish off.
Gather around the edge of the hair piece and attach it to Alistair's head following the instructions on page 21.

BEARD

Alistair's long, straggly beard is created as one row of double loop stitches of varying lengths. For a fuller beard, use triple loop stitch (see page 21).

Using 3.00mm (US 3) needles and light grey yarn, cast on 26 sts.
row 1: LS to end. Vary the amount of yarn used for the loops as follows: first 3 sts use 12cm (4¾in) of yarn; next 3 sts use 32cm (12½in) of yarn; next 8 sts use 60cm (23½in) of yarn; next 3 sts use 32cm (12½in) of yarn; last 3 sts use 12cm (4¾in) of yarn.
Cast off.
Pinch the cast-on and cast-off edges together and sew them to form a narrow strip. Attach the beard to Alistair's chin, meeting the hairline on both sides of his head.

EYEBROWS

Make two.

Using 2.25mm (US 1) needles and the light grey yarn, cast on 8 sts.
row 1: TLS to end of row.
Cast off.

Sew the eyebrows to the face, just above the eyes. Cut the loops and trim them to the desired length. Separate the strands of yarn for a softer look.

NOSE

Using 2.25 (US 1) needles and flesh-coloured yarn, cast on 8 sts.
row 1: knit.
row 2: purl.
row 3: K2, inc 1 st in next 4 sts, K2 [12 sts].
row 4: purl.
row 5: K5, inc 1 st in next 2 sts, K5 [14 sts].
row 6: purl.

row 7: (K2tog) twice, K6, (K2tog) twice [10 sts].
row 8: P2tog, P6, P2tog [8 sts].
row 9: K2tog, K4, K2tog [6 sts].
row 10: P2tog, P2, P2tog [4 sts].
row 11: (K2tog) twice [2 sts].
row 12: P2tog [1 st].

1. Oversew the edges of the nose from the tip upwards. Fill it slightly as you go. Sew up the remainder of the seam.
2. Sew the top half of the nose to Alistair's face with the top of the nose placed centrally and aligned with the middle of his eyes.

MOUSTACHE

1. Using the same yarn as the beard, put ten 40cm (15¾in) strands of yarn together and tie securely in the middle.
2. Attach the moustache to Alistair's face, just above the mouth.
3. Trim single strands of the moustache to vary their length and create a more 'straggly' look.
4. Secure the moustache on either side of the face, approximately 1cm (½in) from the nose, using two strands of yarn taken from the beard.

HAT

Using 3.00mm (US 3) needles and purple yarn, cast on 60 sts.
rows 1–4: GS, commencing with a knit row.
row 5: K5, (K10, K2tog) 5 times, K5 [55 sts].
rows 6–10: SS, commencing with a purl row.
row 11: K5, (K9, K2tog) 5 times, K4 [50 sts].
rows 12–16: SS, commencing with a purl row.
row 17: K4, (K8, K2tog) 5 times, K4 [45 sts].
rows 18–22: SS, commencing with a purl row.
row 23: K4, (K7, K2tog) 5 times, K3 [40 sts].
rows 24–28: SS, commencing with a purl row.
row 29: K3, (K6, K2tog) 5 times, K3 [35 sts].
rows 30–34: SS, commencing with a purl row.
row 35: K3, (K5, K2tog) 5 times, K2 [30 sts].
rows 36–40: SS, commencing with a purl row.
row 41: K2, (K4, K2tog) 5 times, K2 [25 sts].
rows 42–46: SS, commencing with a purl row.
row 47: K2, (K3, K2tog) 5 times, K1 [20 sts].
rows 48–52: SS, commencing with a purl row.
row 53: K1, (K2, K2tog) 5 times, K1 [15 sts].
rows 54–58: SS, commencing with a purl row.

row 59: (K1, K2tog) 5 times [10 sts].
rows 60–64: SS, commencing with a purl row.
row 65: (K2tog) 5 times [5 sts].
rows 66–70: SS, commencing with a purl row.
row 71: (K2tog) twice, K1 [3 sts].
row 72: purl.
row 73: K2tog, K1 [2 sts].
row 74: P2tog.

Break yarn, leaving a good length to sew up the side of the hat, and pull through the last stitch. Finish off. Sew up the edges of the hat and sew in the loose ends. Embroider stars and moons on to the hat, using yellow yarn. For the moons, use a loose, curved, uneven stem stitch.

TIES

Alistair has problems keeping his hat on, especially in the wind, so Elizabeth Witch showed him how she uses ribbons to secure her hat. Of course, Alistair calls his hat fastenings 'ties'.

Make two.

Using 3.00mm (US 3) needles and the same colour yarn as you used for the hair, cast on 5 sts.
row 1: knit.
row 2: cast off 1 st, knit to end [4 sts].
row 3: knit.
row 4: Cast off 1 st, knit to end [3 sts].
row 5: knit.
row 6: Cast off 1 st, knit to end [2 sts].
rows 7–50: GS.
Cast off, leaving enough yarn to sew the ties to Alistair's hat. Sew in the other loose end.

TUNIC

Alistair's tunic is knitted in two colours: the main colour, lilac (M) and the contrasting colour, yellow (C).

FRONT AND BACK

Using 3.00mm (US 3) needles and M, cast on 60 sts.
rows 1–10: GS.
rows 11–16: change to C, GS.
rows 17–20: change to M, GS.
row 21: (K10, K2tog) twice, K12, (K2tog tbl, K9) twice [56 sts].
rows 22–28: SS, commencing with a purl row.
row 29: (K9, K2tog) twice, K12, (K2tog tbl, K9) twice [52 sts].
rows 30–36: SS, commencing with a purl row.
row 37: (K8, K2tog) twice, K12, (K2tog tbl, K8) twice [48 sts].
rows 38–44: SS, commencing with a purl row.
row 45: (K7, K2tog) twice, K12, (K2tog tbl, K7) twice [44 sts].
rows 46–52: SS, commencing with a purl row.
row 53: (K6, K2tog) twice, K12, (K2tog tbl, K6) twice [40 sts].
rows 54–60: SS, commencing with a purl row.
row 61: (K6, K2tog) twice, K8, (K2tog tbl, K6) twice [36 sts].
rows 62–67: SS, commencing with a purl row.
row 68: (K5, K2tog) twice, K8, (K2tog tbl, K5) twice [32 sts].
rows 69–74: SS, commencing with a purl row.
row 75: K5, K2tog, K18, K2tog tbl, K5 [30 sts].
rows 76–81: SS, commencing with a purl row.
Mark each end of row 81 with waste yarn to indicate the beginning of the armhole.
rows 82–95: SS, commencing with a purl row.
rows 96–99: GS.
row 100: K8, cast off 14 sts, K8.
rows 101–105: GS, using the last 8 sts.
Cast off.
Rejoin yarn to remaining 8 sts.
With WS facing, GS for 5 rows.
Cast off.

The collar, shown in a different colour for clarity, before making up.

row 3: K7, sl1, turn.
row 4: ytb, sl1, K7.
row 5: K6, sl1, turn.
row 6: ytb, sl1, K6.
row 7: K5, sl1, turn.
row 8: ytb, sl1, K5.
row 9: K4, sl1, turn.
row 10: ytb, sl1, K4.
row 11: K3, sl1, turn.
row 12: ytb, sl1, K3.
row 13: K2, sl1, turn.
row 14: ytb, sl1, K2.
row 15: K1, sl1, turn.
row 16: ytb, sl1, K1.
row 17: inc 1 st in each of the following 7 sts, K49.
rows 18–31: repeat rows 3–16.
row 32: inc 1 st in each of the following 7 sts, K28, sl1, turn.
row 33: ytb, sl1, K14, sl1, turn.
row 34: ytb, sl1, K13, sl1, turn.
row 35: ytb, sl1, K12, sl1, turn.
row 36: ytb, sl1, K11, sl1, turn.
row 37: ytb, sl1, K10, sl1, turn.
row 38: ytb, sl1, K9, sl1, turn.
row 39: ytb, sl1, K8, sl1, turn.
row 40: ytb, sl1, K7, sl1, turn.
row 41: ytb, sl1, K6, sl1, turn.
row 42: ytb, sl1, K5, sl1, turn.
row 43: ytb, sl1, K4, sl1, turn.
row 44: ytb, sl1, K3, sl1, turn.
row 45: ytb, sl1, K2, sl1, turn.
row 46: ytb, sl1, K1, sl1, turn, ytb, sl1.
row 47: inc 1 st in each of the following 7 sts, K28.
Break yarn.
row 48: slip 42 sts on to RH needle. Rejoin yarn. Inc 1 st in each of the following 7 sts, K28.
rows 49–56: GS.
Cast off and sew in the loose ends.

Making up

Sew in the loose ends. Sew the shoulder seams together. Sew the sides of the tunic from the hem to the beginning of the armholes.

COLLAR

The collar is knitted separately and in one piece, commencing at the neck edge.
Using 3.00mm (US 3) needles and lilac yarn, cast on 56 sts.
Row 1 is a WS row.
rows 1–2: GS.

Attaching the collar

Make a flat seam at the side edges of the collar. This becomes the centre back of the collar. Place the collar inside the tunic with RS facing. Pin the collar and oversew the edges to form a flat seam, matching the centre back of the collar with the centre back of the tunic.

SLEEVES

Make two.

Cast on 36 sts.
rows 1–6: SS, commencing with a knit row.
row 7: K2tog, knit to last 2 sts, K2tog tbl [34 sts].
rows 8–12: SS, commencing with a purl row.
rows 13–30: repeat rows 7–12, 3 times [28 sts].
row 31: K2tog, knit to last 2 sts, K2tog tbl [26 sts].
row 32: purl.

Change to 2.25mm (US 1) needles.
rows 33–42: rib (K1, P1) to end.
row 43: inc 1 st in every st [52 sts].
Cast off.

Attaching the sleeves

Sew the sleeve edges together. For each sleeve, with RS facing, sew sleeve to armhole of tunic, matching the sleeve seam to the bottom of the armhole.

BELTS

Make two twisted cords (see page 12) with three strands of yarn in yellow, purple and lilac, each 108cm (42½in) long. After twisting, knot one end leaving 2cm (¾in) of spare yarn as a tassle. Wrap both cords around Alistair's tunic and pass the tassles through the loops made at the other end to secure.

The completed tunic.

row 9: K2tog, K18, K2tog, K16, K2tog, K18, K2tog [56 sts].
row 10: knit.
rows 11–16: change to C, GS.
row 17: K2tog, K16, K2tog, K16, K2tog, K16, K2tog [52 sts].
row 18: knit.
rows 19–22: change to M, GS.
rows 23–24: SS, commencing with a knit row.
row 25: K2tog, K15, K2tog, K14, K2tog, K15, K2tog [48 sts].
rows 26–32: SS, commencing with a purl row.
row 33: K2tog, K14, K2tog, K12, K2tog, K14, K2tog [44 sts].
rows 34–40: SS, commencing with a purl row.
row 41: K2tog, K12, K2tog, K12, K2tog, K12, K2tog [40 sts].
rows 42–48: SS, commencing with a purl row.
row 49: K2tog, K11, K2tog, K10, K2tog, K11, K2tog [36 sts].
rows 50–56: SS, commencing with a purl row.
row 57: K2tog, K9, K2tog, K10, K2tog, K9, K2tog [32 sts].
rows 58–64: SS, commencing with a purl row.
row 65: cast off 3 sts, knit to end [29 sts].
row 66: cast off 3 sts, purl to end [26 sts].
row 67: K2tog, knit to last 2 sts, K2tog [24 sts].
rows 68–84: SS, commencing with a purl row.

Change to 2.25mm (US 1) needles.
rows 85–86: (K1, P1) to end.
row 87: K1, (yrn, K2tog) to last st, yrn, K1 [25 sts].
row 88: (K1, P1) to last st, K1.
Cast off ribwise, loosely.

MAKING UP

1. Sew the edge of the legs together. Slip one leg inside the other, RS facing, and sew up the front and back body seams.
2. Make a chain cord or twisted cord (see page 12) for the waistline. Thread the cord through the eyelet holes, commencing at the centre front.

PANTS

Alistair's pants, like his tunic, are knitted in two colours, though this time the main colour (M) is yellow and the contrasting colour (C) is lilac.

LEGS AND BODY

Make two.

Using 3.00mm (US 3) needles and M, cast on 60 sts.
rows 1–8: GS (row 1 is RS row).

CLOAK

Alistair's cloak starts with 200 stitches, so you will need a long pair of 3.00mm (US 3) needles, at least 30cm (11¾in) in length, until you get to a more comfortable number of stitches that will fit on to shorter needles.

Alistair's cloak is knitted mainly in one piece, with the sleeves and wide edging at the front knitted separately and attached once the main body of the cloak is complete. The draping effect at the back of the cloak is created using partial knitting.

Using a long pair of 3.00mm (US 3) needles and purple yarn, cast on 200 sts (you may wish to put a marker every 50 stitches or so).

row 1: K110, sl1, turn.
row 2: ytb, sl1, K20, sl1, turn.
row 3: ytb, sl1, K30, sl1, turn.
row 4: ytb, sl1, K40, sl1, turn.
row 5: ytb, sl1, K50, sl1, turn.
row 6: ytb, sl1, K60, sl1, turn.
row 7: ytb, sl1, K70, sl1, turn.
row 8: ytb, sl1, K80, sl1, turn.
row 9: ytb, sl1, K90, sl1, turn.
row 10: ytb, sl1, K100, sl1, turn.
row 11: ytb, sl1, K110, sl1, turn.
row 12: ytb, sl1, K120, sl1, turn.
row 13: ytb, sl1, K130, sl1, turn.

row 14: ytb, sl1, K140, sl1, turn.
row 15: ytb, sl1, K150, sl1, turn.
row 16: ytb, sl1, K160, sl1, turn.
row 17: ytb, sl1, K170, sl1, turn.
row 18: ytb, sl1, K180, sl1, turn.
row 19: ytb, sl1, K190, sl1, turn.
row 20: K200.
rows 21–36: GS.
row 37: K10 (right front edging), put these sts on to a stitch holder and knit across remaining sts [190 sts].
row 38: K10 (left front edging), put these sts on to a stitch holder and purl across remaining sts [180 sts].

SHAPING THE WAISTLINE

row 39: (K16, K2tog) 4 times, K11, K2tog, K10, K2tog tbl, K11, (K2tog tbl, K16) 4 times [170 sts].
rows 40–44: SS, commencing with a purl row.
row 45: (K15, K2tog) 4 times, K10, K2tog, K10, K2tog tbl, K10, (K2tog tbl, K15) 4 times [160 sts].
rows 46–50: SS, commencing with a purl row.
row 51: (K14, K2tog) 4 times, K10, K2tog, K8, K2tog tbl, K10, (K2tog tbl, K14) 4 times [150 sts].
rows 52–56: SS, commencing with a purl row.
row 57: (K13, K2tog) 4 times, K9, K2tog, K8, K2tog tbl, K9, (K2tog tbl, K13) 4 times [140 sts].
rows 58–62: SS, commencing with a purl row.
row 63: (K12, K2tog) 4 times, K8, K2tog, K8, K2tog tbl, K8, (K2tog tbl, K12) 4 times [130 sts].
rows 64–68: SS, commencing with a purl row.
row 69: (K11, K2tog) 4 times, K7, K2tog, K8, K2tog tbl, K7, (K2tog tbl, K11) 4 times [120 sts].
rows 70–74: SS, commencing with a purl row.
row 75: (K10, K2tog) 4 times, K7, K2tog, K6, K2tog tbl, K7, (K2tog tbl, K10) 4 times [110 sts].
rows 76–80: SS, commencing with a purl row.
row 81: (K9, K2tog) 4 times, K6, K2tog, K6, K2tog tbl, K6, (K2tog tbl, K9) 4 times [100 sts].
rows 82–86: SS, commencing with a purl row.
row 87: (K8, K2tog) 4 times, K5, K2tog, K6, K2tog tbl, K5, (K2tog tbl, K8) 4 times [90 sts].
rows 88–92: SS, commencing with a purl row.
row 93: (K7, K2tog) 4 times, K5, K2tog, K4, K2tog tbl, K5, (K2tog tbl, K7) 4 times [80 sts].
rows 94–98: SS, commencing with a purl row.
row 99: (K6, K2tog) 4 times, K4, K2tog, K4, K2tog tbl, K4, (K2tog tbl, K6) 4 times [70 sts].
rows 100–104: SS, commencing with a purl row.
row 105: (K5, K2tog) 4 times, K3, K2tog, K4, K2tog tbl, K3, (K2tog tbl, K5) 4 times [60 sts].
rows 106–110: SS, commencing with a purl row.
row 111: (K4, K2tog) 4 times, K3, K2tog, K2, K2tog tbl, K3, (K2tog tbl, K5) 4 times [50 sts].
row 112: purl.
row 113: K22, K2tog, K2, K2tog tbl, K22 [48 sts].
row 114: purl.
row 115: knit.
Break the yarn. Put these 48 sts on to a stitch holder.

FRONT EDGING

With WS facing, put the 10 sts of the right front edging on to a 3.00mm (US 3) needle.
Rejoin yarn.
Knit 100 rows.
Put sts on to a stitch holder. Break yarn.
With RS facing, put the 10 sts of the left front edging on to a 3.00mm (US 3) needle.
Rejoin yarn.
Knit 101 rows.

row 116: with WS facing, knit 10 sts (of left front edging). Put the 48 sts of the back bodice on to a needle and purl 48 sts. Put remaining 10 sts (of right front edging) from the stitch holder on to a needle and knit 10 sts [68 sts].

Tip

All yarn rejoins are to the inside seam stitches.
This avoids any sewing in of loose ends on the edge of the front edgings.

RIGHT FRONT EDGING AND RIGHT FRONT OF BODICE

With RS facing:
row 117: K18, turn.
Continue with these 18 sts (remaining 50 sts can be put on to a stitch holder).
row 118: P8, K10.
rows 119–144: repeat rows 117 and 118, 13 times.
row 145: repeat row 117.

Shoulder shaping

row 146: cast off 8 sts, K10.

Shaping collar back edge

rows 147–166: GS.
Cast off (this is centre back of collar).
Sew in loose ends.

BACK OF BODICE

Put 32 sts of the 50 sts previously held on a stitch holder on to a needle. This leaves 18 sts for the left front edge.
With RS facing, rejoin yarn.
rows 117–140: SS.
row 141: K8, turn.
rows 142–146: SS, commencing with a purl row.
Cast off.
With RS facing, rejoin yarn.
row 141: cast off 16 sts, (with 1 st on needle) K7.
rows 142–146: SS, commencing with a purl row.
Cast off.

LEFT FRONT EDGING AND LEFT FRONT OF BODICE

With RS facing:
Put remaining 18 sts on to LH needle.
Rejoin yarn.
row 117: K18.
row 118: K10, P8.
rows 119–144: repeat rows 117 and 118, 13 times.

Shoulder shaping

row 145: cast off 8 sts, K10.

Shaping collar back edge

rows 146–165: GS.
Cast off (this is centre back of collar). Sew in loose ends.
This side of the cloak is 1 row shorter than than the right side to allow for rejoining of yarn on inside of garment sts.

SLEEVES

Make two.

Using 3.00mm (US 3) needles, cast on 60 sts.
GS for 16 rows.
SS for 28 rows, decreasing 1 st at each end of the sixth and every following sixth row until 48 sts remain.
SS for 8 rows, commencing with a knit row.
Cast off.

MAKING UP

Make all the seams as flat as possible.
1. Sew the front edgings to the front body of the cloak.
2. Sew the shoulder seams.

3. Sew the cast-off edges of the collar together. Remember that the RS of the collar is on the inside of the cloak, because the collar folds over the neckline. Sew the collar to the neckline edge.
4. Sew the edges of the sleeves together.
5. With RS facing, sew the sleeves to the armholes, matching the sleeve seams to the bottom of the armhole, and the centre top of the sleeve to the shoulder seam. Turn up the cuff.
6. Embroider stars and moons, randomly, over the cloak.

Close-up of the sleeve, made up.

SHOES

Make two.

SOLE

Using yellow yarn and 2.25mm (US 1) needles, cast on 1 st.
row 1: (RS row) inc in this st [2 sts].
row 2: knit.
row 3: inc in first st, K1 [3 sts].
row 4: inc in first st, K2 [4 sts].
rows 5–12: GS for 8 rows.
row 13: K1, inc in next st, K2 [5 sts].
row 14: K1, inc in next st, K3 [6 sts].
rows 15–22: GS.
row 23: K1, inc in next st, K4 [7 sts].
row 24: K1, inc in next st, K5 [8 sts].
rows 25–28: GS.
row 29: K1, inc in next st, K6 [9 sts].
row 30: K1, inc in next st, K7 [10 sts].
rows 31–49: GS.
row 50: K2tog, K6, K2tog tbl [8 sts].
row 51: knit.
row 52: K2tog, K4, K2tog tbl [6 sts].
row 53: knit.
Cast off.

TOP

Using purple yarn and 2.25mm (US 1) needles, cast on 1 st.
Repeat rows 1–30 of the sole [10 sts].
row 31: K1, inc in next st, K8 [11 sts].
row 32: K1, inc in next st, K9 [12 sts].
row 33: K1, inc in next st, K10 [13 sts].
row 34: K1, inc in next st, K11 [14 sts].
rows 35–39: GS.
row 40: K7, turn.
Put remaining 7 sts on to a stitch holder or leave on needle.
rows 41–59: GS.
Cast off.
Replace held sts on to a needle and rejoin yarn, or simply rejoin
yarn to remaining sts on needle.
rows 40–60: GS.
Cast off.
With RS facing, commencing at the back heel edge, pick up and
knit 15 sts to the centre of the shoe and another
15 sts for the other side [30 sts].
row 1: K14, inc in next 2 sts, K14 [32 sts].
row 2: K15, inc in next 2 sts, K15 [34 sts].
row 3: K16, inc in next 2 sts, K16 [36 sts].
row 4: K17, inc in next 2 sts, K17 [38 sts].
row 5: K18, inc in next 2 sts, K18 [40 sts].
row 6: K19, inc in next 2 sts, K19 [42 sts].
row 7: K20, inc in next 2 sts, K20 [44 sts].
row 8: K21, inc in next 2 sts, K21 [46 sts].
row 9: K22, inc in next 2 sts, K22 [48 sts].
row 10: K23, inc in next 2 sts, K23 [50 sts].
Cast off loosely, or use a larger needle. Sew in loose ends.

MAKING UP

Oversew the heel edges, remembering that the seam reverses
at the cuff so that it can be folded outwards. Oversew the top of
the shoe to the sole.

SANDALS

LEFT SANDAL

Make two. Reverse the pattern for the right sandal.

Cast on 14 sts (this is the front of the sandal).
rows 1–6: (K1, P1) rib (this is the wide strap that fits over the
front of the foot).
row 7: cast off 2 sts, K3, cast off 4 sts, K5.
row 8: cast off 2 sts, K3, turn. Put remaining sts on to
a stitch holder.
rows 9–23: GS (this is one of the side straps).
The work should now be RS facing.
Cast on 3 sts.
rows 24–29: GS.
row 30: cast off 3 sts, K3.
rows 31–45: GS.

Make a bobble button: K1, knit 3 sts into next st, turn, K3, turn,
K3tog, K1. Finish off by threading yarn through remaining sts and
sew into the beginning of the button, creating a bobble. Rejoin
yarn to remaining 3 sts and create a loop through the sts, large
enough to secure the button. Buttonhole stitch around the loop.

SOLE

Make four.

Cast on 4 sts.
row 1: inc in first st, K1, inc in next st, K1 [6 sts].
row 2: inc in first st, K3, inc in next st, K1 [8 sts].
rows 3–32: GS.
row 33: K2tog, K6 [7 sts].
row 34: K2tog, K5 [6 sts].
row 35: K2tog, K4 [5 sts].
Cast off.

MAKING UP

Sew two soles together for each shoe (this makes a good, firm
sole). Sew the top edges of the sandal to the sole, beginning at
the sixth row. Sew the heel strap edge to the centre back of
the sole.

Santa Claus

As you can see, with just a simple change of colour you can make a completely new character to add to your collection. Here, I have taken elements from Alistair Wizard and Samuel Crowe Pirate and knitted them in red and white yarn to create this gorgeous Santa Claus. The cloak is based on Alistair's cloak, to which I have added large pockets that have been filled with a few tiny toys. Santa's pants are a shorter version of the wizard's, and the wizard's hat has also been adapted by adding a jolly white pompom. The shirt, boots and belt are borrowed from Samuel Crowe.

Materials and equipment

As for Alistair.

Yarns (approximate amounts):
100g (3½oz) cream/flesh coloured for basic body
200g (7oz) red for cloak, hat and pants
140g (4¾oz) white for shirt, hair, beard and edgings
small amounts of black for boots and belt, black, white, red and blue for face, and grey for buckle

FACE

Copy Santa's face from the photograph, or create your own following the guidelines on page 19. Colour his cheeks and the tip of his nose with a touch of pink chalk or crayon.

NOSE

Using 2.25mm (US 1) needles, cast on 7 sts.
row 1: knit.
row 2: P2tog, P3, P2tog tbl [5 sts].
row 3: K2tog, K1, K2tog tbl [3 sts].
row 4: purl.

row 5: K2tog, K1, pass first st over second st.
Finish off.
Sew the edges and stuff the nose. Oversew the base of the nose and sew it to face.

HAIR

Using white yarn, follow the basic instructions on pages 20–21 to create Santa's curly hair. Each loop is made by wrapping the yarn once around two fingers.

BEARD

Using 2.25mm (US 1) needles and white yarn, cast on 26 sts.
row 1: TLS to end.
row 2: knit.
row 3: TLS to end.
Cast off.
Turn in the cast-off edge and sew the beard to the face, meeting the hairline at each side and placing the beard just below Santa's mouth.

MOUSTACHE

1. Place together ten strands of white yarn approximately 40cm (15¾in) long and secure them in the middle with a length of waste yarn.
2. Pin the centre of the moustache to the face, just under the nose. Twist each side of the moustache to shape it and pin it in place to the sides of the face.
3. Sew the moustache to Santa's face to secure it, sewing in each of the ten strands. Take the ends through to the back of the head.

PANTS

Using 3.00mm (US 3) needles and white yarn, cast on 48 sts.
rows 1–10: moss stitch.
Change to red.
rows 11–12: SS, commencing with a knit row.
Complete as for Alistair Wizard's pants, from row 33 onwards (see page 77).

CLOAK

Follow the cloak pattern for Alistair Wizard (see pages 78–80), using white for the edging and cuffs and red for the cloak. Add a large pocket on either side and replace the sleeve pattern with the one below:

SLEEVES

Make two.

Using 3.00mm (US 3) needles and red yarn, cast on 48 sts.
rows 1–44: SS.
Change to white.
row 45: purl.
rows 46–72: moss stitch.
Cast off in pattern.
Turn up the white cuff.

POCKETS

Make two.

Using red yarn, cast on 28 sts.
rows 1–22: SS.
Change to white.
rows 23–27: moss stitch.
Cast off in pattern.
Sew the pockets to the front of the cloak, using the photograph for reference. Make the top of the pocket baggier than the bottom so that it hangs open, allowing the tiny toys placed inside to be seen.

BELT

Follow the pattern for Samuel Crowe's belt (see page 66), knitting it in black yarn and the buckle in grey.

BOOTS

Following the pattern for Samuel Crowe's boots, use black yarn and 2.25mm (US 1) needles to complete the two soles.
For the legs, omit rows 1–24.
row 25: K2, inc in next st, (K4, inc in next st) 5 times, K2 [36 sts].
rows 26–29: GS.
row 30: K3, inc in next st, (K4, inc in next st) 6 times, K2 [43 sts].
rows 31–34: GS.
Cast off loosely, or use a size larger needle.
Sew the back seam of the leg, keeping in mind that the top of the boot turns over. Oversew the GS rows and mattress stitch the SS rows down to the heel position.

HAT

Knit the wizard's hat (see pages 73–74) in red and white yarn, replacing the first four rows with moss stitch worked in white. Omit the embroidery and add a white pompom to the point of the hat.

SHIRT

Follow Samuel Crowe's shirt pattern (see pages 62–64).

Place tiny treasures in Santa's pockets. These are made from single strands of green and red yarn threaded with tiny Christmas beads.

85

Princess Neridah

Princess Neridah's clothes suit her sweet, romantic nature perfectly. Her strappy undertop and long, embroidered pants are worn under a simple underskirt and top skirt. The shorter top skirt has a lacey hem that finishes just above the scallop-edged hem of her underskirt, and the pretty matching jacket, with its rather regal lace-pointed ruff and puffed sleeves, gives a rich, layered look to Neridah's outfit.

With great pride Princess Neridah wears her long flowing cloak, with patterned sleeves and wrap-around pointed collar. It is longer at the back than the front and flows behind her as she walks, reminding everyone that she is, after all, a princess, and likes to dress as one. Princess Neridah does not have pockets so she takes her matching pineapple purse with her when she goes shopping – usually for flowers and ribbons to put in her hair. She also likes visiting Elizabeth Witch, and she just has room in her purse for a few moonbeams, some stardust and a handful of wishes to take home with her.

Dainty ankle-strap shoes poke their toes out from under her skirts when she walks, and Neridah also likes to wear a choker necklace and ring to complete her outfit. In her blonde, wavy hair she wears ribbons in colours that match her clothes or, on more formal occasions, a sparkly tiara.

Begin by knitting the basic body for your doll (see pages 14–18).

Materials and equipment

Needles: two pairs of 3.00mm (US 3), one long and one short, and one pair of 2.25mm (US 1)

Crochet hook: 3.00mm (US 0)

Stitch holders and optional 2.25mm (US 1) double-pointed needles

Needle with eye large enough for yarn, e.g. tapestry needle

Bead-headed pins

Small, self-adhesive pink gemstones for decorations on bag

Silver glitter glue for decorating tiara

Two white chenille sticks, approximately 27cm (10¾in) long

Filling: the best quality polyester filling that you can buy

Yarns (approximate amounts):
100g (3½oz) cream/flesh coloured for basic body
350g (12¼oz) white for clothes
80g (2¾oz) various shades of light brown for hair
small amounts of pink and green for embroidery and ribbons, and black, white, pink and green for face

V-PATTERN

The V-pattern is used on much of Neridah's clothing. With a number of V-patterns to knit, I found it easier to place the Vs on to a double-pointed needle, where I could make sure I had them in the correct order for joining them all together and, of course, all facing the same way.

yon (yarn over needle) at the beginning of a row increases one stitch and makes a little loop. The K2tog (knit two together) takes the extra stitch away again.
yfwd (yarn forward) increases one stitch and becomes part of the lace pattern.

Cast on 1 st.
row 1: (WS row) inc 1 st in first st [2 sts].
row 2: knit.
row 3: yon, K2 [3 sts].
row 4: yon, K1, yfwd, K2 [5 sts].
row 5: yon, K2tog, P1, K2.
row 6: yon, K2tog, knit to end.
row 7: yon, K2tog, P1, K2.
row 8: yon, K2tog, yfwd, K1, yfwd, K2 [7 sts].
row 9: yon, K2tog, K1, P1, K3.

row 10: yon, K2tog, knit to end.
row 11: yon, K2tog, K1, P1, K3.
row 12: yon, K2tog, yfwd, K1, yfwd, K2tog, yfwd, K2 [9 sts].
row 13: yon, K2tog, K2, P1, K4.
row 14: yon, K2tog, knit to end.
row 15: yon, K2tog, K2, P1, K4.
row 16: yon, K2tog, yfwd, K1, yfwd, K2tog, yfwd, K2tog tbl, yfwd, K2 [11 sts].
row 17: yon, K2tog, K2, P3, K4.
row 18: yon, K2tog, knit to end.
row 19: yon, K2tog, K2, P3, K4.
row 20: yon, K2tog, yfwd, K1, yfwd, K2tog, K2, yfwd, K2tog tbl, yfwd, K2 [13 sts].
row 21: yon, K2tog, K2, P5, K4.
row 22: yon, K2tog, knit to end.
row 23: yon, K2tog, K2, P5, K4.
row 24: yon, K2tog, yfwd, K2, yfwd, K2tog, K2, yfwd, k2tog tbl, K1, yfwd, K2 [15 sts].
row 25: yon, K2tog, K2, P2, K3, P2, K4.
row 26: yon, K2tog, knit to end.
row 27: yon, K2tog, K2, P2, K3, P2, K4.

FACE

Create Neridah's face following the photograph on the left and the instructions on page 19.

HAIR

Follow the instructions for the basic hair piece on pages 20–21, looping the yarn around four fingers twice to create the loops. Leave the loops uncut.

RIBBON

Make Neridah's hair ribbon from 30cm (11¾in) lengths of green, pink and white yarn. Knot the ends, put them together and tie them around her head. Make a single, simple knot. Create an even prettier hair decoration by also tying each separate piece of yarn in a tiny bow. Alternatively, use crocheted chains, twisted cords or a plait to decorate Neridah's hair.

On more formal occasions, Neridah wears a tiara (see pages 104–105).

TOP SKIRT

Using 3.00mm (US 3) needles and white yarn, complete eleven V-patterns, each one knitted up to and including row 23. Each V-pattern ends with 13 sts, making a total of 143 sts when multiplied by 11. Break the yarn after each V-pattern and place on to double-pointed needles. On the last V-pattern, do not break the yarn. Sew in the loose ends as you work to make the knitting easier to handle.

With all the V-patterns on the LH needle, and with RS facing:
row 1: (K2, yfwd, K2tog, K2, yfwd, K2tog, K1, K2tog tbl, yfwd, K2) 11 times [143 sts].
row 2: (K3, P7, K3) 11 times.
row 3: knit.
row 4: K2, (P9, K4) 10 times, P9, K2.
row 5: knit.
row 6: P1, (K2, P7, K2, P2) 10 times, K2, P7, K2, P1.
row 7: knit.
row 8: P2, (K2, P5, K2, P4) 10 times, K2, P5, K2, P2.
row 9: knit.
row 10: P3, (K2, P3, K2, P6) 10 times, K2, P3, K2, P3.

Neridah's, top skirt is worn over her longer underskirt. The sumptuous layers, delicate lace edging and pretty rosebuds are perfect for this beautiful princess.

row 11: knit.
row 12: P4, (K2, P1, K2, P8) 10 times, K2, P1, K2, P4.
row 13: knit.
row 14: P5, (K3, P10) 10 times, K3, P5.
row 15: knit.
row 16: P6, (K1, P12) 10 times, K1, P6.
row 17: K6, (K2tog, K11) 10 times, K2tog, K5 [132 sts].
rows 18–20: SS, starting with a purl row.
row 21: K5, (K2tog, K10) 10 times, K2tog, K5 [121 sts].
rows 22–24: SS, starting with a purl row.
row 25: K4, (K2tog, K9) 10 times, K2tog, K5 [110 sts].

The completed top skirt.

rows 26–28: SS, starting with a purl row.
row 29: K4, (K2tog, K8) 10 times, K2tog, K4 [99 sts].
rows 30–34: SS, starting with a purl row.
row 35: K3, (K2tog, K7) 10 times, K2tog, K4 [88 sts].
row 36–40: SS, starting with a purl row.
row 41: K3, (K2tog, K6) 10 times, K2tog, K3 [77 sts].
row 42–46: SS, starting with a purl row.
row 47: K2, (K2tog, K5) 10 times, K2tog, K3 [66 sts].
row 48–52: SS, starting with a purl row.
row 53: K2, (K2tog, K4) 10 times, K2tog, K2 [55 sts].
rows 54–58: SS, starting with a purl row.

Change to 2.25mm (US 1) needles.
row 59: rib (K1, P1) to end.
row 60: K1, (yfwd, K2tog) to last st, K1.
row 61: rib (K1, P1) to end.
Cast off ribwise.

MAKING UP

1. Sew the skirt edges together leaving 4cm (1½in) at the waistline for ease of fit. This is the back seam.
2. Make a cord and thread through the eyelet holes, commencing at the back seam. Alternatively, thread elastic through the holes for an elasticated waist.
3. Embroider rosebuds at the top of the diamond shapes, or apply your own creative embellishments.

ROSEBUDS

Thread a needle with pink yarn and bring it through to the front of the knitting where you wish to position the rosebud. Make a stitch 0.5cm (¼in) long and bring the tip of the needle back through at the point at which you started. Wind the yarn around the needle 5–7 times and gently pull the needle through to form a bullion knot. Work three or four more stitches in the same way to form a small, compact rose shape. Change to green yarn, and work three chain stitches around the rosebud.

The detailing on the top skirt.

UNDERSKIRT

Using 3.00mm (US 3) needles and white yarn, cast on 145 sts.
rows 1–15: SS, commencing with a knit row.
row 16: K2, (yfwd, K2tog) to last st, K1 (picot hemline).
row 17: knit.
row 18: K2, (P11, K2) 11 times.
row 19: knit.
row 20: K3, (P9, K4) 10 times, P9, K3.
row 21: knit.
row 22: K1, P1, (K2, P7, K2, P2) 10 times, K2, P7, K2, P1, K1.
row 23: knit.
row 24: K1, P2, (K2, P5, K2, P4) 10 times, K2, P5, K2, P2, K1.
row 25: knit.
row 26: K1, P3, (K2, P3, K2, P6) 10 times, K2, P3, K2, P3, K1.
row 27: knit.
row 28: K1, P4, (K2, P1, K2, P8) 10 times, K2, P1, K2, P4, K1.
row 29: knit.
row 30: K1, P5, (K3, P10) 10 times, K3, P5, K1.
row 31: knit.
row 32: K1, P6, (K1, P12) 10 times, K1, P6, K1.
rows 33–42: SS, commencing with a knit row.
row 43: K6, K2tog, (K11, K2tog) 10 times, K7 [134 sts].
rows 44–52: SS, commencing with a purl row.
row 53: K6, K2tog, (K10, K2tog) 10 times, K6 [123 sts].
rows 54–62: SS, commencing with a purl row.
row 63: K5, K2tog, (K9, K2tog) 10 times, K6 [112 sts].
rows 64–72: SS, commencing with a purl row.
row 73: K5, K2tog, (K8, K2tog) 10 times, K5 [101 sts].
rows 74–82: SS, commencing with a purl row.
row 83: K4, K2tog, (K7, K2tog) 10 times, K5 [90 sts].
rows 84–88: SS, commencing with a purl row.
row 89: K4, K2tog, (K6, K2tog) 10 times, K4 [79 sts].
row 90: purl.
row 91: K2, (K2tog, K1) 25 times, K2 [54 sts].

Princess Neridah, in her pretty underskirt and sleeveless undertop – perfect for warm, summer evenings.

Change to 2.25mm (US 1) needles for the waistline.
row 92: rib (K1, P1) to end.
row 93: K1, (yfwd, K2tog) to last st, yfwd, K1 (eyelet holes for waist cord) [55 sts].
row 94: rib (K1, P1) to end.
Cast off.

MAKING UP

1. Sew up the edges of the skirt to within 4cm (1½in) of the waistline. This makes it easier to dress and undress your doll. Thread a cord (or elastic) through the eyelet holes.
2. Embroider rosebuds and leaves at the tip of the zigzag pattern along the hem of the skirt, or apply your own creative embellishments.
3. Turn the hem at the picot line and sew it in place.

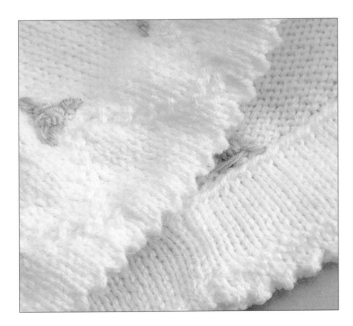

Detailing on hem of underskirt.

The completed jacket (front)

JACKET

The hem of Neridah's jacket is made up of seven V-patterns:

two 9-stitch V-patterns (completed up to and including row 15) [9 sts].

two 11-stitch V-patterns (completed up to and including row 19) [11 sts].

two 13-stitch V-patterns (completed up to and including row 23) [13 sts].

one 15-stitch V-pattern (completed up to and including row 27) [15 sts].

Arrange the V-patterns, RS facing, on to double-pointed needles in the following order: 9-stitch, 11-stitch, 13-stitch, 15-stitch, 13-stitch, 11-stitch and 9-stitch. Do not break the yarn of the last V-pattern [81 sts].

Keeping the tension firm, join the V-patterns:
row 1: (RS row) yon, K2tog, knit to end.
row 2: yon, K2tog, K2, P3, K4, P7, K4, P9, K4, P11, K4, P9, K4, P7, K4, P3, K4 [81 sts].
row 3: yon, K2tog, K2, yfwd, K2tog, K8, yfwd, K2tog, K10, yfwd, K2tog, K12, yfwd, K2tog, K12, yfwd, K2tog, K10, yfwd, K2tog, K8, yfwd, K2tog, K3.
row 4: yon, K2tog, K2, P2, K2, P2, K2, P5, K2, P2, K2, P7, K2, P2, K2, P9, K2, P2, K2, P7, K2, P2, K2, P5, K2, P2, K2, P2, K4.
row 5: yon, K2tog, knit to end.
row 6: yon, K2tog, K2, P1, K2, P4, K2, P3, K2, P4, K2, P5, K2, P4, K2, P7, K2, P4, K2, P5, K2, P4, K2, P3, K2, P4, K2, P1, K4.
row 7: yon, K2tog, knit to end.
row 8: yon, K2tog, K4, P6, K2, P1, K2, P6, K2, P3, K2, P6, K2, P5, K2, P6, K2, P3, K2, P6, K2, P1, K2, P6, K6.
row 9: yon, K2tog, knit to end.
row 10: yon, K2tog, K3, P8, K3, P8, K2, P1, K2, P8, K2, P3, K2, P8, K2, P1, K2, P8, K3, P8, K5.

The completed jacket (back)

row 11: yon, K2tog, knit to end.
row 12: yon, K2tog, K2, P10, K1, P10, K3, P10, K2, P1, K2, P10, K3, P10, K1, P10, K4.
row 13: yon, K2tog, knit to end.
row 14: yon, K2tog, K2, P22, K1, P12, K3, P12, K1, P22, K4.
row 15: yon, K2tog, knit to end.
row 16: yon, K2tog, K2, P36, K1, P36, K4 [81 sts].
row 17: yon, K2tog, K10, K2tog, K1, K2tog tbl, K7, K2tog, K1, K2tog tbl, K9, K2tog, K1, K2tog tbl, K9, K2tog, K1, K2tog tbl, K7, K2tog, K1, K2tog tbl, K12 [71 sts].
row 18: yon, K2tog, K2, purl to last 4 sts, K4.
row 19: yon, K2tog, K9, K2tog, K1, K2tog tbl, K5, K2tog, K1, K2tog tbl, K7, K2tog, K1, K2tog tbl, K7, K2tog, K1, K2tog tbl, K5, K2tog, K1, K2tog tbl, K11 [61 sts].
row 20: yon, K2tog, K2, purl to last 4 sts, K4.
row 21: yon, K2tog, K8, K2tog, K1, K2tog tbl, K3, K2tog, K1, K2tog tbl, K5, K2tog, K1, K2tog tbl, K5, K2tog, K1, K2tog tbl, K3, K2tog, K1, K2tog tbl, K10 [51 sts].

row 22: yon, K2tog, K2, purl to last 4 sts, K4.
Change to 2.25 (US 1) needles.
row 23: yon, K2tog, knit to end.
row 24: yon, K2tog, K2, purl to last 4 sts, K4.
rows 25–26: repeat rows 23 and 24.

Change to 3.00mm (US 3) needles.
row 27: yon, K2tog, K2, K2tog, knit to last 6 sts, K2tog tbl, K4 [49 sts].
row 28: yon, K2tog, K2, purl to last 4 sts, K4.
row 29: yon, K2tog, knit to end.
row 30: repeat row 28.
row 31: yon, K2tog, K2, K2tog, knit to last 6 sts, K2tog tbl, K4 [47 sts].
row 32: repeat row 28.

Neridah, in her gorgeous jacket and skirts.

BODICE

The first 11 sts on your needle will be used for the right front of the bodice, the middle 25 sts will be used for the back, and the remaining 11 sts will be used for the left front.

Right front of bodice

With RS facing:
row 33: yon, K2tog, K9, turn [11 sts]
(The remaining sts can be put on to a stitch holder.)
row 34: P7, K4.
row 35: yon, K2tog, K2, K2tog, K5 [10 sts].
row 36: P6, K4.
row 37: yon, K2tog, K8.

row 38: P6, K4.
row 39: yon, K2tog, K2, K2tog, K4 [9 sts].
row 40: P5, K4.
row 41: yon, K2tog, K7.
row 42: P5, K4.
row 43: yon, K2tog, K2, K2tog, K3 [8 sts].
row 44: P4, K4.
row 45: yon, K2tog, K6.
row 46: P4, K4.
row 47: yon, K2tog, K2, K2tog, K2 [7 sts].
row 48: P3, K4.
row 49: yon, K2tog, K5.
row 50: P3, K4.
row 51: yon, K2tog, K5.
row 52: P3, K4.
Cast off.

Back of bodice

Using the 25 back bodice sts (if necessary, put these back on to needle from stitch holder) and with RS facing, rejoin yarn.
rows 33–46: SS, commencing with a knit row.

To shape the neckline:
row 47: K9, cast off 7 sts, (with 1 st on needle) K8 [9 sts].
Using the last 9 sts:
row 48: P7, P2tog [8 sts].
row 49: K2tog tbl, K6 [7 sts].
rows 50–52: SS, commencing with a purl row.
Cast off.
With WS facing, rejoin yarn to other 9 sts.
row 48: P2tog, P7 [8 sts].
row 49: K6, K2tog [7 sts].
rows 50–52: SS, commencing with a purl row.
Cast off.

Left front of bodice

Using the remaining 11 sts (if necessary, put these back on to needle from stitch holder) and with RS facing, rejoin yarn.
row 33: K11.
row 34: yon, K2tog, K2, P7.
row 35: K5, K2tog tbl, K4 [10 sts].
row 36: yon, K2tog, K2, P6.
row 37: K10.
row 38: yon, K2tog, K2, P6.
row 39: K4, K2tog tbl, K4 [9 sts].
row 40: yon, K2tog, K2, P5.
row 41: K9.
row 42: yon, K2tog, K2, P5.
row 43: K3, K2tog tbl, K4 [8 sts].
row 44: yon, K2tog, K2, P4.
row 45: K8.
row 46: yon, K2tog, K2, P4.
row 47: K2, K2tog tbl, K4 [7 sts].
row 48: yon, K2tog, K2, P3.
row 49: K7.

row 50: yon, K2tog, K2, P3.
row 51: K7.
row 52: yon, K2tog, K2, P3.
Cast off.
Sew in loose ends and sew shoulder seams together.

COLLAR

Mark a point 2cm (¾in) from the shoulder seam down each side of the front edging.

Using 3.00mm (US 3) needles and with RS facing, pick up and knit the following stitches around the neck edge, starting at the marker: 5 sts to the shoulder seam, 16 sts around the back neck edge and another 5 sts from the shoulder seam to the other marker [26 sts].
SS for 5 rows, commencing with a purl row.
next row: K1, (yfwd, K2tog) to last st, yfwd, K1.
Cast off loosely and sew in loose ends.
This collar rolls away from the neck edge naturally.
When attaching the neck ruff, tuck it under the collar.

RUFF

Complete one V-pattern up to and including row 19 [11 sts] and four V-patterns up to and including row 15 [9 sts]. With RS facing, put the V-patterns together on a 3.00mm (US 3) needle with the largest V-pattern in the middle [47 sts].
Keeping the tension firm, join the V-patterns:
row 1: yon, K2tog, knit to end.
row 2: yon, K2tog, K2, (K2tog) to last 3 sts, K3 [27 sts].
Cast off loosely.
With RS together, pin the ruff to the neck edge, under the roll of the collar. Sew the ruff to the neck edge.

SLEEVES

Make two.

Complete four V-patterns up to and including row 11 [7 sts].
Sew in the loose ends as you go.
With RS facing, put the four V-patterns together on a 3.00mm (US 1) needle [28 sts].
row 1: knit.

row 2: knit.
row 3: K1, (yfwd, K1) to last st, K1 [54 sts].
rows 4–28: SS for 25 rows, commencing with a purl row.
row 29: K1, (K2tog) to last st, K1 [26 sts].
row 30: purl.
row 31: knit.
row 32: purl.
Cast off loosely and sew the edges of the sleeve together.

Make a chain cord or twisted cord using pink, green and white yarn and thread it through the eyelet holes, beginning and ending at the outside centre of the sleeve. When fitting the jacket to your doll, tighten the cord, tie it in a bow and puff up the sleeve.

MAKING UP

Sew up the side seams of the jacket and turn the jacket inside-out. Place the sleeves inside the jacket armholes, with RS together. Match the sleeve seams to the underarm of the bodice. Pin the sleeves to the jacket and sew them in place.

BUTTON AND LOOP FASTENING

Using 2.25mm (US 1) needles and white yarn, cast on 3 sts.
row 1: inc in each st [6 sts].
rows 2–5: knit.
row 6: (K2tog) to end [3 sts].
Cast off. Thread the yarn around the edge of the work, gather it tightly and finish off.

1. Attach the button to the right-hand edge of the jacket at the waist.
2. Make a double loop with the yarn, big enough to secure the button, and buttonhole stitch around the loop. Attach the finished loop to the other side of the jacket.

CLOAK

Neridah's cloak commences with a larger number of stitches than usual and will require needles at least 30cm (11¾in) in length until you have decreased down to about 100 stitches. The front, edges, back and collar are knitted in one piece and the sleeves are knitted separately.

The back edging consists of 20 rows of garter stitch, and the draping effect is created by partial knitting.

Using long, 3.00mm (US 3) needles and white yarn, cast on 200 sts. To make counting your stitches easier, you may wish to put a marker every 50 stitches or so.

row 1: K110, sl1, turn.
row 2: ytb, sl1, K20, sl1, turn.
row 3: ytb, sl1, K30, sl1, turn.
row 4: ytb, sl1, K40, sl1, turn.
row 5: ytb, sl1, K50, sl1, turn.
row 6: ytb, sl1, K60, sl1, turn.
row 7: ytb, sl1, K70, sl1, turn.
row 8: ytb, sl1, K80, sl1, turn.
row 9: ytb, sl1, K90, sl1, turn.
row 10: ytb, sl1, K100, sl1, turn.
row 11: ytb, sl1, K110, sl1, turn.
row 12: ytb, sl1, K120, sl1, turn.
row 13: ytb, sl1, K130, sl1, turn.
row 14: ytb, sl1, K140, sl1, turn.
row 15: ytb, sl1, K150, sl1, turn.
row 16: ytb, sl1, K160, sl1, turn.
row 17: ytb, sl1, K170, sl1, turn.
row 18: ytb, sl1, K180, sl1, turn.
row 19: ytb, sl1, K190, knit to end.
row 20: K200.
rows 21–36: GS for 16 rows.
row 37: K10 (right front edging). Put these sts on to a stitch holder and knit across remaining sts [190 sts].
row 38: K10 (left front edging). Put these sts on to a stitch holder and purl across remaining sts [180 sts].

Back view of cloak.

Side view of cloak.

SHAPING THE WAISTLINE

row 39: (K16, K2tog) 4 times, K11, K2tog, K10, K2tog tbl, K11, (K2tog tbl, K16) 4 times [170 sts].

rows 40–44: SS, commencing with a purl row.

row 45: (K15, K2tog) 4 times, K10, K2tog, K10, K2tog tbl, K10, (K2tog tbl, K15) 4 times [160 sts].

rows 46–50: SS, commencing with a purl row.

row 51: (K14, K2tog) 4 times, K10, K2tog, K8, K2tog tbl, K10, (K2tog tbl, K14) 4 times [150 sts].

rows 52–56: SS, commencing with a purl row.

row 57: (K13, K2tog) 4 times, K9, K2tog, K8, K2tog tbl, K9, (K2tog tbl, K13) 4 times [140 sts].

rows 58–62: SS, commencing with a purl row.

row 63: (K12, K2tog) 4 times, K8, K2tog, K8, K2tog tbl, K8, (K2tog tbl, K12) 4 times [130 sts].

rows 64–68: SS, commencing with a purl row.

row 69: (K11, K2tog) 4 times, K7, K2tog, K8, K2tog tbl, K7, (K2tog tbl, K11) 4 times [120 sts].

rows 70–74: SS, commencing with a purl row.

row 75: (K10, K2tog) 4 times, K7, K2tog, K6, K2tog tbl, K7, (K2tog tbl, K10) 4 times [110 sts].

rows 76–80: SS, commencing with a purl row.

row 81: (K9, K2tog) 4 times, K6, K2tog, K6, K2tog tbl, K6, (K2tog tbl, K9) 4 times [100 sts].

rows 82–86: SS, commencing with a purl row.

row 87: (K8, K2tog) 4 times, K5, K2tog, K6, K2tog tbl, K5, (K2tog tbl, K8) 4 times [90 sts].

rows 88–92: SS, commencing with a purl row.

row 93: (K7, K2tog) 4 times, K5, K2tog, K4, K2tog tbl, K5, (K2tog tbl, K7) 4 times [80 sts].

rows 94–98: SS, commencing with a purl row.

row 99: (K6, K2tog) 4 times, K4, K2tog, K4, K2tog tbl, K4, (K2tog tbl, K6) 4 times [70 sts].

rows 100–104: SS, commencing with a purl row.

row 105: (K5, K2tog) 4 times, K3, K2tog, K4, K2tog tbl, K3, (K2tog tbl, K5) 4 times [60 sts].

rows 106–110: SS, commencing with a purl row.

row 111: (K4, K2tog) 4 times, K3, K2tog, K2, K2tog tbl, K3, (K2tog tbl, K4) 4 times [50 sts].

row 112: purl.

row 113: K22, K2tog, K2, K2tog tbl, K22 [48 sts].

row 114: purl.

row 115: knit.

Break the yarn. Put these 48 sts on to a stitch holder.

FRONT EDGING

With WS facing, put the 10 sts of the right front edging on to a 3.00mm (US 3) needle.

Rejoin the yarn.

GS for 100 rows.

Break yarn and put the sts on to a stitch holder.

With RS facing, put the 10 sts of the left front edging on to a 3.00mm (US 3) needle.

Rejoin yarn.

GS for 101 rows.

row 116: With WS facing, knit 10 sts (of left front edging). Put the 48 sts of the back bodice on to a needle and purl 48 sts. Put remaining 10 sts (of right front edging) from the stitch holder on to a needle and knit 10 sts [68 sts].

Note that all yarn rejoins are to the inside seam stitches. This avoids any sewing in of loose ends on the edge of the front edgings.

As garter stitch knits up to a different tension from stocking stitch, the edging rows are not counted in the main body of the work.

When the edgings are knitted across with the body, row 116 is created.

RIGHT FRONT EDGING AND RIGHT FRONT OF BODICE

With RS facing:

row 117: K18, turn.

Continue with these 18 sts (remaining 50 sts can be put on to a stitch holder).

row 118: P8, K10.

row 119: K18.

rows 120–133: repeat rows 118 and 119, 7 times.

row 134: P8, K1, inc in next st, K8 [19 sts].

row 135: cast on 1 st, K20 [20 sts].

row 136: P8, K1, inc in next st, K10 [21 sts].

row 137: cast on 1 st, K22 [22 sts].

row 138: P8, K1, inc in next st, K12 [23 sts].

row 139: cast on 1 st, K24 [24 sts].

row 140: P8, K1, inc in next st, K14 [25 sts].

row 141: cast on 1 st, K26 [26 sts].

row 142: P8, K1, inc in next st, K16 [27 sts].

row 143: cast on 1 st, K28 [28 sts].

row 144: P8, K1, inc in next st, K18 [29 sts].

row 145: cast on 1 st, K30 [30 sts].

Shoulder shaping

row 146: cast off 8 sts purlwise, knit to end [22 sts].

These 22 sts are used for the collar back.

Shaping collar back edge

row 147: Cast off 1 st, knit to end [21 sts].

row 148: knit.

rows 149–156: repeat rows 147 and 148, 4 times [17 sts].

row 157: cast on 1 st, knit to end [18 sts].

row 158: knit.

rows 159–168: repeat rows 157 and 158, 5 times [23 sts].

Cast off. This cast-off edge is the centre back of the collar.

BACK OF BODICE

Put held sts on to a needle.

With RS facing, rejoin yarn.

row 117: K32, turn.

These 32 sts form the bodice back. Put remaining sts on to a stitch holder.

rows 118–140: SS, commencing with a purl row.

row 141: K8, turn.

rows 142–146: SS, commencing with a purl row.

Cast off.

With RS facing, rejoin yarn.

row 141: cast off 16 sts, (with 1 st on needle) K7.

rows 142–146: SS, commencing with a purl row.

Cast off.

Back and right front, before making up.

LEFT FRONT EDGING AND LEFT FRONT OF BODICE

Put remaining 18 sts held on stitch holder on to a needle.
With RS facing, rejoin yarn.
row 117: knit.
row 118: K10, P8.
row 119: knit.
rows 120–133: repeat rows 118 and 119, 7 times.
row 134: K10, P8.
row 135: K8, K1, inc in next st, K8 [19 sts].
row 136: cast on 1 st, K12, P8 [20 sts].
row 137: K8, K1, inc in next st, K10 [21 sts].
row 138: cast on 1 st, K14, P8 [22 sts].
row 139: K8, K1, inc in next st, K12 [23 sts].
row 140: cast on 1 st, K16, P8 [24 sts].
row 141: K8, K1, inc in next st, K14 [25 sts].
row 142: cast on 1 st, K18, P8 [26 sts].
row 143: K8, K1, inc in next st, K16 [27 sts].
row 144: cast on 1 st, K20, P8 [28 sts].
row 145: K8, K1, inc in next st, K18 [29 sts].
row 146: cast on 1 st, K22, P8 [30 sts].

Shoulder shaping

row 147: cast off 8 sts, knit to end [22 sts].
These 22 sts are used for the collar back.

Shaping collar back edge

row 148: cast off 1 st, knit to end [21 sts].
row 149: knit.
rows 150–157: repeat rows 148 and 149, 4 times [17 sts].
row 158: cast on 1 st, knit to end [18 sts].
row 159: knit.
rows 160–169: repeat rows 158 and 159, 5 times [23 sts].
Cast off. This cast-off edge is the centre back of the collar.
Sew in the loose ends.

SLEEVES

The full sleeves of Neridah's cloak allow room for her jacket sleeves underneath. The ribbons around the wrists are tied into bows. The lacey sleeve edge finishes at row 31, after which the knitting loosens a little.

Make two.

Using 3.00mm (US 3) needles and white yarn, cast on 1 st.
row 1: inc in first st [2 sts].
row 2: knit.
row 3: yon, K2 [3 sts].
row 4: yon, K1, yfwd, K2 [5 sts].
row 5: yon, K2tog, yfwd, K1, yfwd, K2 [7 sts].
row 6: yon, K2tog, knit to end.
row 7: yon, K2tog, yfwd, inc in next st, K1, inc in next st, yfwd, K2 [11 sts].
row 8: yon, K2tog, knit to end.
row 9: yon, K2tog, yfwd, inc in next st, K5, inc in next st, yfwd,

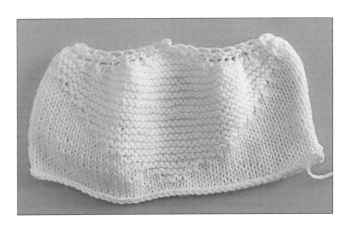

A sleeve, before making up.

K2 [15 sts].
row 10: yon, K2tog, knit to end.
row 11: yon, K2tog, yfwd, inc in next st, K9, inc in next st, yfwd, K2 [19 sts].
row 12: yon, K2tog, knit to end.
row 13: yon, K2tog, yfwd, inc in next st, K13, inc in next st, yfwd, K2 [23 sts].
row 14: yon, K2tog, knit to end.
row 15: yon, K2tog, yfwd, inc in next st, K17, inc in next st, yfwd, K2 [27 sts].
row 16: yon, K2tog, knit to end.
row 17: yon, K2tog, yfwd, inc in next st, K21, inc in next st, yfwd, K2 [31 sts].
row 18: yon, K2tog, knit to end.
row 19: yon, K2tog, yfwd, inc in next st, K25, inc in next st, yfwd, K2 [35 sts].
row 20: yon, K2tog, knit to end.
row 21: yon, K2tog, yfwd, inc in next st, K29, inc in next st, yfwd, K2 [39 sts].
row 22: yon, K2tog, knit to end.
row 23: yon, K2tog, yfwd, inc in next st, K33, inc in next st, yfwd, K2 [43 sts].
row 24: yon, K2tog, knit to end.
row 25: yon, K2tog, yfwd, inc in next st, K37, inc in next st, yfwd, K2 [47 sts].
row 26: yon, K2tog, knit to end.
row 27: yon, K2tog, yfwd, inc in next st, K41, inc in next st, yfwd, K2 [51 sts].
row 28: yon, K2tog, knit to end.
row 29: yon, K2tog, yfwd, inc in next st, K45, inc in next st, yfwd, K2 [55 sts].
row 30: yon, K2tog, knit to end.
row 31: yon, K2tog, yfwd, inc in next st, K49, inc in next st, yfwd, K2 [59 sts].
row 32: knit.
row 33: P6, K47, P6.
row 34: knit.
row 35: P2tog, P6, K43, P6, P2tog [57 sts].
row 36: knit.
row 37: P9, K39, P9.
row 38: knit.

row 39: P2tog, P9, K35, P9, P2tog [55 sts].
row 40: knit.
row 41: P12, K31, P12.
row 42: knit.
row 43: P2tog, P12, K27, P12, P2tog [53 sts].
row 44: knit.
row 45: P15, K23, P15.
row 46: knit.
row 47: P2tog, P15, K19, P15, P2tog [51 sts].
row 48: knit.
row 49: P18, K15, P18.
row 50: knit.
row 51: P2tog, P18, K11, P18, P2tog [49 sts].
row 52: knit.
row 53: P21, K7, P21.
row 54: knit.
row 55: P2tog, P21, K3, P21, P2tog [47 sts].
row 56: knit.
row 57: purl.
Cast off. Sew in loose ends.

MAKING UP

Make all the seams as flat as possible.
1. Sew the front edgings to the front body of the cloak.
2. Sew the shoulder seams.
3. Sew the cast-off edges of the collar together. Remember that the RS of the collar is on the inside of the cloak, because the collar folds over the neckline. Sew the collar to the neckline edge.
4. Sew the edges of the sleeves together.
5. With RS facing, sew the sleeves to the armholes, matching the sleeve seams to the bottom of the armhole, and the centre top of the sleeve to the shoulder seam.
6. Thread three strands of pink, green and white yarn through the eyelet holes at the wrist, commencing at the centre point of the sleeve. Tie each coloured yarn into a separate bow.
7. Embroider the cloak with rosebuds and leaves.

PANTS

Make two lace edgings, one for each leg.

Cast on 3 sts using 3.00mm (US 3) needles and white yarn.
row 1: (WS row) knit.
row 2: yon, K2tog, K1 [3 sts].
row 3: K1, yfwd, K2 [4 sts].
row 4: yon, K2tog, K2.
row 5: K2, yfwd, K2 [5 sts].
row 6: yon, K2tog, K3.
row 7: K3, yfwd, K2 [6 sts].
row 8: yon, K2tog, K4.
row 9: K2, yfwd, K2tog, K2tog [5 sts].
row 10: yon, K2tog, K3.
row 11: K2, yfwd, K2tog, K1 [5 sts].
row 12: yon, (K2tog) twice, K1 [4 sts].
row 13: K1, K2tog, K1 [3 sts].
row 14: yon, K2tog, K1 [3 sts].
Repeat rows 1–14, 4 times.
Cast off.

Close-up of back of cloak and sleeve, made up.

LEGS

First leg

row 1: with RS facing, pick up 45 sts along the straight edge of the lace edging.
row 2: purl.
row 3: (K2, yfwd) to last 2 sts, K2 [44 sts].
rows 4–34: SS, commencing with a purl row.
Break yarn and put sts on to a stitch holder.

Second leg

Repeat rows 1–34 (first leg).
row 35: knit across 45 sts of second leg then put held sts of first leg on to needle and knit across [90 sts].
row 36: purl.
rows 37–52: SS, commencing with a purl row.
row 53: K1, (K2tog) to last st, K1 [44 sts].

Change to 2.25mm (US 1) needles.
row 54: rib (K1, P1) to end.
row 55: rib (P1, K1) to end.
row 56: K1, (yfwd, K2tog) to last st, yfwd, K1 [45 sts].
row 57: rib (K1, P1) to last st, K1.
row 58: cast off ribwise.

MAKING UP

1. Sew up the seams of each leg and the back seam of the body, finishing 4cm (1½in) from the waistline.
2. Make a cord for the waist (see page 12). Thread the cord through the eyelet holes commencing from the centre back.
3. Cut three lengths of yarn in white, pink and green. Put a knot at the end of each piece and thread them through the eyelet holes at the bottom of the pants, starting at the outside edge. Tie each length of yarn in a seperate knot.
4. Add rosebud embroideries to each leg where indicated.

UNDERTOP

This little top is knitted sideways.

Using 3.00mm (US 3) needles and white yarn, cast on 18 sts.
row 1: knit.
row 2: yon, K2tog, purl to last 3 sts, K3.
row 3: knit.
row 4: yon, K2tog, purl to last 3 sts, K3.
row 5: knit.
row 6: yon, K2tog, knit to end.
repeat rows 1–6, 10 times.
Cast off.
Sew the cast-on and cast-off edges together. This seam becomes the centre back seam. The looped stitch edge is at the top of the garment.

STRAPS

Make two.

Cast on 3 sts.
Knit 30 rows.
Cast off.

Attach the straps to the bodice below the looped stitches, 2cm (¾in) and 7cm (2¾in) from the back seam.

Princess Neridah loves the detailing on her matching pants and undertop.

SHOES

SOLE

Make two.

Using 2.25mm (US 1) needles, cast on 5 sts.
row 1: (RS row) knit.
row 2: inc in first st, K2, inc in next st, K1 [7 sts].
rows 3–14: GS.
row 15: inc in first st, K4, inc in next st, K1 [9 sts].
rows 16–27: GS.
row 28: K1, K2tog, K3, K2tog tbl, K1 [7 sts].
rows 29–34: GS.
row 35: K1, K2tog, K1, K2tog tbl, K1 [5 sts].
rows 36–39: GS.
row 40: K2tog, K1, K2tog tbl [3 sts].
row 41: K2tog, K1 [2 sts].
row 42: K2tog [1 st].
Finish off. Sew in loose ends.

INSTEP AND SIDES

Make two.

Cast on 56 sts. Leave approximately 50cm (19¾in) of waste yarn for sewing up.
row 1: (RS row) K2tog, knit to last 2 sts, K2tog tbl [54 sts].
row 2: K2tog, K10, sl1, turn, ytb, sl1, K9, K2tog tbl [52 sts].
row 3: K2tog, K6, sl1, turn, ytb, sl1, K5, K2tog tbl [50 sts].
row 4: K2tog, knit to last 2 sts, K2tog tbl [48 sts].
rows 5–6: repeat rows 2 and 3 [44 sts].
row 7: K2tog, K8, K2tog, K8, K2tog, K2tog tbl, K8, K2tog tbl, K8, K2tog tbl [38 sts].
row 8: cast off, knitting first 2 sts tog and last 2 sts tog tbl.
Finish off. Leave approximately 30cm (11¾in) of waste yarn for sewing up.

ANKLE STRAPS

Make two.

Leave approximately 30cm (11¾in) of waste yarn at the beginning of the strap for sewing the bobble button.

Cast on 3 sts.
row 1: inc in each st [6 sts].
row 2: knit.
row 3: (K2tog) 3 times [3 sts].
row 4: K2tog, K1 [2 sts].
rows 5–44: GS.
row 45: K1, (yrn) twice, K1.
row 46: K1, knit into loop once, K1 [3 sts].
row 47: K2tog, K1 [2 sts].
row 48: K2tog [1 st].
Finish off.

Use the waste yarn at the beginning of the strap to make small gathering stitches around the shape made for the button by the first 3 rows. Pull the yarn tightly to make the bobble button and finish off.

MAKING UP

1. Place instep edges (WS) together and oversew the instep edge. Pin the sides of the shoe to the sole, matching the toe points and heels. With RS on the outside, oversew the edges, catching half a stitch from the sole and the upper.

2. Sew the straps to the heels with one strap fastening to the RHS of the shoe and the other to the LHS. Oversew 1cm (½in) of strap to the centre back of the heel.

RING

Make a double loop with white yarn, big enough to go around one of Neridah's fingers. Buttonhole stitch around the loop, and then sew a number of smaller loops using pink, white and green yarn on to one edge of the ring.

PINEAPPLE PURSE

Princess Neridah does not have pockets in her skirts or jacket, so when she goes shopping she likes to take her purse. The top of the purse is gathered together, making it look like a pineapple.

rows 1–12: using 3.00mm (US 3) needles, make 5 V-patterns, following rows 1–12 inclusive of the pattern on page 88.
With WS facing, put all the V-patterns on to the LH needle.
rows 13–14: knit [45 sts].
row 15: purl.
row 16: K1, (K2tog, yfwd) to last 2 sts, K2.
row 17: purl.
rows 18–19: GS.
rows 20–22: SS, commencing with a purl row.
row 23: (bubble stitch row) K2, (knit into front and then into back of next st, turn, P2, turn, K2, pass second st over first st, K4) 8 times, knit into front and then into back of next st, turn, P2, turn, K2, pass second st over first st, K2.
rows 24–26: SS, commencing with a purl row.
row 27: (bubble stitch row) K4, (knit into back and then into front of next st, turn, P2, turn, K2, pass second st over first st) 8 times, K3, knit into back and then into front of next st, turn, P2, turn, K2, pass second st over first st, K1.
rows 28–30: SS, commencing with a purl row.
row 31: repeat row 23.
rows 32–35: SS, commencing with a purl row.
rows 36–38: SS, commencing with a knit row.
row 39: knit.
row 40: K1, (K2tog, K3) 8 times, K2tog, K2 [36 sts].

row 41: purl.
row 42: K1, (K2tog, K2) 8 times, K2tog, K1 [27 sts].
row 43: purl.
row 44: K1, (K2tog, K1) 8 times, K2tog [18 sts].
row 45: purl.
row 46: K1, (K2tog) 8 times, K1 [10 sts].
row 47: purl.
row 48: (K2tog) to end [5 sts].
Thread yarn through remaining 5 sts, pull tightly and finish off. Sew the row ends together. Decorate with tiny, self-adhesive gemstones.

Make two cords (see page 12). Thread each cord through the eyelet holes, starting each one on opposite sides of the purse, to create a drawstring bag.

TIARA

Twist two chenille sticks together, each approximately 27cm (10¾in) long. Form them into a ring, twisting 1cm (½in) at each end together to secure.

Using 3.00mm (US 3) needles, knit 1 small V-pattern up to and including row 9 (see page 88). Leave these 7 sts on your needle. Break yarn.
Cast on 1 st and knit a larger V-pattern up to and including row 13. Leave these 9 sts on your needle. You should now have 16 sts on your LH needle.
Break yarn.

The pineapple purse is shown here together with a smaller, plainer version of similar design.

Cast on 1 st and knit another small V-pattern up to and including row 9 [23 sts].
With RS facing, cast on 8 sts [31 sts].
next row: knit across all sts.
next row: cast on 8 sts, purl to end [39 sts].
SS for 6 rows, commencing with a knit row.
Cast off loosely.

MAKING UP

The stocking stitch forms a natural roll in the knitting, with the purlside on the outside. Join the edges to form a circle and place the chenille wire ring inside it. Wrap the knitting around the wire ring, keeping the V-patterns pointing upwards. Embellish with glitter glue or, alternatively, self-adhesive gemstones.

CHOKER NECKLACE

With white yarn and a 3.00mm (US 0) crochet hook, make a chain to fit the neckline of your doll.

BUTTON

Cast on 3 sts.
row 1: inc in each st [6 sts].
rows 2–5: knit.
row 6: (K2tog) to end [3 sts].
Cast off.
Thread the yarn around the edge of the work, gather it tightly and finish off.

FINISHING OFF

1. Attach the button to one end of the necklace.
2. Make a double loop with the yarn, big enough to secure the button, and buttonhole stitch around the loop. Attach the loop to the other side of the necklace.
3. Embroider a tiny rosebud with leaves on to the necklace at the front.

Neridah's delicate choker necklace matches her pink rosebud lips and green eyes.

Victoria

Simply changing the main colour, once again, makes a big difference to the look and appeal of your doll. Victoria's cloak is shorter than Neridah's to give a wide, draping peplum, and the fluffy trim adds a contrasting texture. Rolled sleeves replace the original cloak sleeves, and readymade fabric rosebuds replace the embroidered rosebuds that enhance Princess Neridah's costume. A metallic thread has been used to embroider the undertop and has also been incorporated into Victoria's jewellery and the ribbons of her jacket sleeves.

Tip

The rosebuds I used were on a thin wire stem. To attach them, I twisted the wire close to the bud into a loop to allow the buds to be sewn on to the costume, and snipped off the excess wire.

Materials and equipment

Needles: two pairs of 3.00mm (US 3), one long and one short, and one pair of 2.25mm (US 1)

Crochet hook: 3.00mm (US 0)

Stitch holders and optional 2.25mm (US 1) double-pointed needles

Needle with eye large enough for yarn, e.g. tapestry needle

Bead-headed pins

Small, self-adhesive lilac gemstones for decorations on dress

Readymade fabric rosebuds

Metallic multicoloured thread

Fluffy lilac trim

Filling: the best quality polyester filling that you can buy

Yarns (approximate amounts):
100g (3½oz) cream/flesh coloured for basic body
150g (5¼oz) white for skirts, jacket and pants
200g (7oz) lilac for coat, undertop and shoes
80g (2¾oz) various shades of lilac for hair
small amounts of black, white, pink and lilac for face

FACE

Copy the face from the photograph shown below, or create your own following the guidance on page 19.

HAIR

Follow the pattern for the basic hair piece on pages 20–21. Make each loop by wrapping it once around four fingers.

JEWELLERY

A simple twisted yarn cord (see page 12), made from lilac and metallic thread, is used to make the necklace, to which I have added a readymade fabric rosebud.

For the bracelet, make a simple I-cord using metallic thread (see page 13), just long enough to fit around Victoria's wrist, and stitch the two ends together. Her ring consists of three tiny, self-adhesive gemstones attached to the middle finger of her left hand.

Victoria's long, wavy hair is swept back off her face and falls freely down her back. The only adornment she wears sometimes is a ribbon made from metallic thread.

Victoria's bracelet and ring.

UNDERTOP

Victoria's undertop is knitted using the same pattern as Princess Neridah's, but without the straps. Two rows of back stitch are embroidered either side of the front panel using the metallic thread, and the same thread is used to oversew around the top edge.

SHOES

Victoria's shoes are the same as Princess Neridah's, but knitted using lilac yarn and decorated with a cluster of three readymade fabric rosebuds.

PURSE

Follow the pattern for Neridah's pineapple purse, using lilac instead of white yarn.

Victoria's pretty purse and shoes.

row 66: purl.
row 67: (K12, K2tog) 4 times, K8, K2tog, K8, K2tog tbl, K8, (K2tog tbl, K12) 4 times [130 sts].
row 68: purl.
row 69: (K11, K2tog) 4 times, K7, K2tog, K8, K2tog tbl, K7, (K2tog tbl, K11) 4 times [120 sts].
row 70: purl.
row 71: (K10, K2tog) 4 times, K7, K2tog, K6, K2tog tbl, K7, (K2tog tbl, K10) 4 times [110 sts].
row 72: purl.
row 73: (K9, K2tog) 4 times, K6, K2tog, K6, K2tog tbl, K6, (K2tog tbl, K9) 4 times [100 sts].
row 74: purl.
row 75: (K8, K2tog) 4 times, K5, K2tog, K6, K2tog tbl, K5, (K2tog tbl, K8) 4 times [90 sts].
row 76: purl.
row 77: (K7, K2tog) 4 times, K5, K2tog, K4, K2tog tbl, K5, (K2tog tbl, K7) 4 times [80 sts].
row 78: purl.
row 79: (K6, K2tog) 4 times, K4, K2tog, K4, K2tog tbl, K4, (K2tog tbl, K6) 4 times [70 sts].
row 80: purl.
row 81: (K5, K2tog) 4 times, K3, K2tog, K4, K2tog tbl, K3, (K2tog tbl, K5) 4 times [60 sts].
row 82: purl.
row 83: (K4, K2tog) 4 times, K3, K2tog, K2, K2tog tbl, K3, (K2tog tbl, K4) 4 times [50 sts].
row 84: purl.
row 85: K22, K2tog, K2, K2tog tbl, K22 [48 sts].
row 86: purl.
row 87: knit.
Break yarn put these 48 sts on to a stitch holder.

CLOAK

Using long, 3.00mm (US 3) needles and lilac yarn, cast on 200 sts.
rows 1–40: complete rows 1–20 of Neridah's cloak pattern, twice.
rows 41–56: GS.
row 57: K10 (right front edging). Put these sts on to a stitch holder and knit across remaining sts [190 sts].
row 58: K10 (left front edging). Put these sts on to a stitch holder and purl across remaining sts [180 sts].

SHAPING TO WAISTLINE

row 59: (K16, K2tog) 4 times, K11, K2tog, K10, K2tog tbl, K11, (K2tog tbl, K16) 4 times [170 sts].
row 60: purl.
row 61: (K15, K2tog) 4 times, K10, K2tog, K10, K2tog tbl, K10, (K2tog tbl, K15) 4 times [160 sts].
row 62: purl.
row 63: (K14, K2tog) 4 times, K10, K2tog, K8, K2tog tbl, K10, (K2tog tbl, K14) 4 times [150 sts].
row 64: purl.
row 65: (K13, K2tog) 4 times, K9, K2tog, K8, K2tog tbl, K9, (K2tog tbl, K13) 4 times [140 sts].

FRONT EDGING

As garter stitch knits up to a different tension from stocking stitch, the edging rows are not counted in the main body of the work. When the edgings are knitted across with the body, row 88 is created.

With WS facing, put the 10 sts of the right front edging on to a 3.00mm (US 3) needle.
Rejoin yarn.
GS for 42 rows.
Break yarn and put sts on to a stitch holder.
With RS facing, put the 10 sts of the left front edging on to a 3.00mm (US 3) needle.
Rejoin yarn.
GS for 43 rows.
row 88: with WS facing, knit 10 sts (of left front edging). Put the 48 sts of the back bodice on to a needle and purl across these 48 sts. Put remaining 10 sts (of right front edging) from the stitch holder on to a needle and knit across these 10 sts [68 sts].

Shoulder shaping

row 118: cast off 8 sts purlwise, knit to end [22 sts].
These 22 sts are used for the collar back.

Shaping collar back edge

row 119: cast off 1 st, knit to end [21 sts].
row 120: knit.
rows 121–128: repeat rows 119 and 120, 4 times [17 sts].
row 129: cast on 1 st, knit to end [18 sts].
row 130: knit.
rows 131–140: repeat rows 129 and 130, 5 times [23 sts].
Cast off. This cast-off edge is the centre back of the collar.

BACK OF BODICE

Put held sts on to a needle.
With RS facing, rejoin yarn.
row 89: K32, turn.
These 32 sts form the bodice back. Put remaining 18 sts on to a stitch holder.
rows 90–112: SS, commencing with a purl row.

Victoria's cloak, showing how prettily it flares at the back.

RIGHT FRONT EDGING AND RIGHT FRONT OF BODICE

With RS facing:
row 89: K18, turn.
Continue with these 18 sts (remaining 50 sts can be put on to a stitch holder).
row 90: P8, K10.
row 91: K18.
rows 92–105: repeat rows 90 and 91, 7 times.
row 106: P8, K1, inc in next st, K8 [19 sts].
row 107: cast on 1 st, K20 [20 sts].
row 108: P8, K1, inc in next st, K10 [21 sts].
row 109: cast on 1 st, K22 [22 sts].
row 110: P8, K1, inc in next st, K12 [23 sts].
row 111: cast on 1 st, K24 [24 sts].
row 112: P8, K1, inc in next st, K14 [25 sts].
row 113: cast on 1 st, K26 [26 sts].
row 114: P8, K1, inc in next st, K16 [27 sts].
row 115: cast on 1 st, K28 [28 sts].
row 116: P8, K1, inc in next st, K18 [29 sts].
row 117: cast on 1 st, K30 [30 sts].

Shaping the neckline

row 113: K8, turn.
rows 114–118: SS, commencing with a purl row.
Cast off.
With RS facing, rejoin yarn.
row 113: cast off 16 sts, (with 1 st on needle) K7.
rows 114–118: SS, commencing with a purl row.
Cast off.

LEFT FRONT EDGING AND LEFT FRONT OF BODICE

Put remaining 18 sts held on stitch holder on to a needle.
With RS facing, rejoin yarn.
row 89: knit.
row 90: K10, P8.
row 91: knit.
rows 92–105: repeat rows 90 and 91, 7 times.
row 106: K10, P8.
row 107: K8, K1, inc in next st, K8 [19 sts].
row 108: cast on 1 st, K12, P8 [20 sts].
row 109: K8, K1, inc in next st, K10 [21 sts].
row 110: cast on 1 st, K14, P8 [22 sts].
row 111: K8, K1, inc in next st, K12 [23 sts].
row 112: cast on 1 st, K16, P8 [24 sts].
row 113: K8, K1, inc in next st, K14 [25 sts].
row 114: cast on 1 st, K18, P8 [26 sts].
row 115: K8, K1, inc in next st, K16 [27 sts].
row 116: cast on 1 st, K20, P8 [28 sts].
row 117: K8, K1, inc in next st, K18 [29 sts].
row 118: cast on 1 st, K22, P8 [30 sts].

Shoulder shaping

row 119: cast off 8 sts, knit to end [22 sts].
These 22 sts are used for the collar back.

Shaping collar back edge

row 120: cast off 1 st, knit to end [21 sts].
row 121: knit.
rows 122–129: repeat rows 120 and 121, 4 times [17 sts].
row 130: cast on 1 st, knit to end [18 sts].
row 131: knit.
rows 132–141: repeat rows 130 and 131, 5 times [23 sts].
Cast off. This cast-off edge is the centre back of the collar.
Sew in the loose ends.

ARMHOLE EDGES

Victoria's cloak does not have long sleeves, but instead the armholes have rolled edges that allow her beautiful jacket sleeves to be displayed.

With RS facing, pick up 54 sts along the armhole edge.
SS for 7 rows, commencing with a purl row.
Cast off. The work will roll naturally.

Make Victoria's skirts and jacket following the same patterns as for Neridah's clothes. Embellish them with readymade fabric rosebuds, attached at the tops of the V-shapes that make up the jacket and top skirt hems, and in-between the zigzags along the top of the hem on the underskirt. Also add some tiny, self-adhesive gemstones at the tops of the zigzags on the jacket and top skirt, and in-between the rosebuds on the underskirt.

MAKING UP

1. Making the seams as flat as possible, sew the front edgings to the front body of the cloak.
2. Sew the shoulder seams.
3. Sew the cast-off edges of the collar together, remembering that the RS of the collar is on the inside of the cloak, because the collar folds over the neckline. Sew the collar to the neckline edge.
4. Weave fluffy yarn along the garter stitch hem and edging. Stop at the shoulder seam.
5. Sew the fluffy yarn around the edge of the collar.

Index